Circled page numbers means need help on that page.

NEW JERSEY TEST PREP

PARCC Practice Book

Mathematics

Grade 3

ISBN 978-1502462084

CONTENTS

INTRODUCTION
For Parents, Teachers, and Tutors

About the PARCC Assessments

Students in New Jersey will be assessed each year by taking a set of tests known as the PARCC assessments. The two main assessments are the Performance-Based Assessment (PBA) and the End-of-Year Assessment (EOY). This book has two complete PBA practice tests and two complete EOY practice tests. The practice tests have the same format, the same question types, and cover the same skills as the real assessments. Further information on the PBA and the EOY is included in the introduction to each practice test.

Key Features of the PARCC Assessments

The PARCC assessments have key features that students will need to be familiar with, including new question styles and formats. These key features are described below.

- The tests are based on the Common Core State Standards and are strongly focused on showing an in-depth understanding of the skills described in the standards.
- The tests include a wider range of question types. There are more constructed response questions, more rigorous selected response questions, more questions involving advanced tasks, and more questions that involve providing explanations or justifying answers.
- The tests are taken online and include computer-based questions. These involve tasks like ordering numbers, selecting points on a number line or graph, sorting items, completing number sentences and equations, and using fraction models.
- The tests include more multi-step problems, more questions that involve applying skills in real-world contexts, and questions that involve complex procedures.

This book has been specifically designed to prepare students for these key features. The questions have a wide range of formats, including questions that mimic the computer-based formats. The questions are more rigorous and include more advanced tasks. The skills assessed match the PARCC tests, with a greater focus on applying skills and on demonstrating in-depth understanding.

About the Common Core State Standards

The state of New Jersey has adopted the Common Core State Standards. These standards describe the skills that students are expected to have. Student learning is based on these standards, and all the questions on the PARCC assessments assess these standards. Just like the real PARCC assessments, the questions in this book test whether students have the knowledge and skills described in the Common Core State Standards.

INTRODUCTION TO THE PBA PRACTICE TEST
For Parents, Teachers, and Tutors

About the Performance-Based Assessment

The Performance-Based Assessment (PBA) is taken after about 75% of the school year is complete. The PBA focuses on applying skills and concepts to solve problems. The emphasis is on completing multi-step problems and advanced tasks. This test is made up of three different types of items, as described below.

- **Type I** – these items are straightforward selected response or simple computer-based questions. These items are worth 1 or 2 points.

- **Type II** – these items are constructed response questions that involve completing more complex tasks and usually require students to show their work, explain their answer, or provide justifications. These items are worth 3 or 4 points.

- **Type III** – these items are complex constructed response questions that involve modeling or applying skills in real-world contexts. These items are worth 3 or 6 points.

The actual test contains 10 Type I items, 4 Type II items, and 3 Type III items. The practice tests in this book contains more questions of each type, especially more Type II and Type III items. This will ensure that students experience all the types of questions they are likely to encounter on the real test and gain the experience needed to complete more rigorous tasks.

Taking the Test

Just like the real EOY test, the practice test is divided into two sessions. Each session includes 15 questions. On the real test, students are allowed 2 hours to complete each session. To account for the additional questions, students should be allowed 4 hours for each session of the practice test. Students can complete the two sessions on the same day or on different days, but should have a break between sessions.

Calculators and Tools

Students should be provided with a ruler to use on both sessions of the test. Students are not allowed to use a calculator on any session of the PARCC tests, and so should complete all the practice tests without the use of a calculator.

PARCC Performance-Based Assessment

Practice Test 1

Session 1

Instructions

Read each question carefully. For each multiple-choice question, fill in the circle for the correct answer. For other types of questions, follow the directions given in the question.

Some questions may ask you to show your work. Be sure to show your work or explain how you found your answer in the space provided.

You may use a ruler to help you answer questions. You may not use a calculator on this test.

1 Mario buys screws in packets of 6.

If Mario counts the screws in groups of 6, which of these numbers would he count? Circle **all** the numbers he would count.

16   (18)   22   26

(30)   (36)   40   (42)

2 The graph shows how long Jason studied for one week.

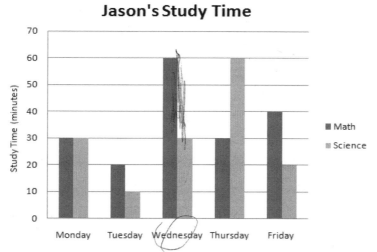

On what day did Jason study science for 30 minutes less than math? Write your answer below.

Wednesday

3 Select **all** the fractions below that are equal to 4.

☑ $\frac{2}{8}$

☐ $\frac{8}{4}$

☐ $\frac{15}{5}$

☑ $\frac{4}{1}$

☑ $\frac{12}{3}$

4 Sally is making a pictograph to show how many students are in grade 3, grade 4, and grade 5.

Grade 3	☺☺☺☺☺☺☺☺☺☺☺
Grade 4	☺☺☺☺☺☺☺☺☺☺☺☺☺☺
Grade 5	

☺ = 5 students

There are 65 students in grade 5. Which of these should Sally use to represent 65 students?

Ⓐ   ☺☺☺☺☺☺☺☺☺☺☺☺

Ⓑ   ☺☺☺☺☺☺☺☺☺☺☺☺☺

Ⓒ   ☺☺☺☺☺☺☺☺☺☺☺☺☺☺

Ⓓ   ☺☺☺☺☺☺☺☺☺☺☺☺☺☺☺

5 Damon rode 3 miles to school every morning, and 3 miles back home each afternoon. How many miles would he ride in 5 days?

    Ⓐ   15 miles

    Ⓑ   30 miles

    Ⓒ   45 miles

    Ⓓ   60 miles

6 Ribbon costs $4 per yard. Allie buys 16 yards of ribbon. Which number sentence could be used to find the total cost of the ribbon, c, in dollars?

    Ⓐ $16 + 4 = c$

    Ⓑ $16 - 4 = c$

    Ⓒ $16 \times 4 = c$

    Ⓓ $16 \div 4 = c = 4$

7 Allen's car has traveled 25,648 miles since it was new. What is this number rounded to the nearest hundred? Write your answer below.

    25,600

8   The school library has 1,532 fiction books, 1,609 non-fiction books, and 1,239 children's books. Complete the number sentence by rounding each number to the nearest hundred and then completing the addition.

$$1,500 + \underline{1,600} + \underline{1,200} = \underline{4,300}$$

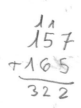

1500
1600
1200
4300

9   There are 157 male students and 165 female students at Ella's school. How many students are there in all?

Ⓐ   322

Ⓑ   312

Ⓒ   222

Ⓓ   212

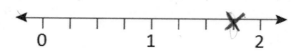

157
+165
322

10   Plot the fraction $1\frac{1}{4}$ on the number line below.

0   1   2

10

11   Look at the group of numbers below. Round each number to the nearest ten. Write your answers below.

108 _110_   864 _860_

87 _90_   196 _200_

282 _280_   35 _40_

981 _980_   773 _770_

On the lines below, explain how you decided whether to round each number up or down.

To round to the nearest 10 1, 2, 3

and 4, the numbers less than 5 do

not round to the 10. 5, 6, 7, 8, 9

are 5 and above can round up 1.

12   During the baseball season, Marvin's team won 5 games and lost 14 games.

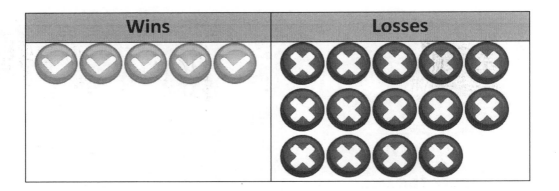

Wins	Losses

What fraction of the total games did the team win?

Show your work.

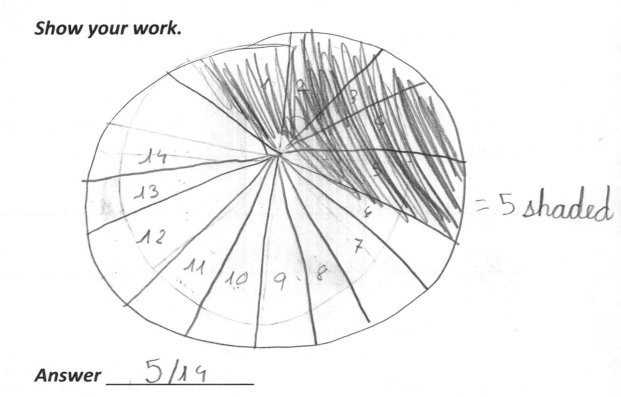

= 5 shaded

Answer   5/19

13   Shade the models below to show $\frac{3}{10}$ and $\frac{1}{5}$.

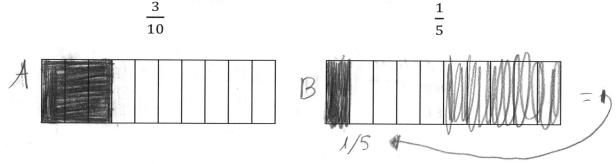

$$\frac{3}{10} \qquad\qquad\qquad \frac{1}{5}$$

Place one of the symbols below in the number sentence to compare the fractions $\frac{3}{10}$ and $\frac{1}{5}$.

$$<, >, =$$

$$\frac{3}{10} \boxed{>} \frac{1}{5}$$

On the lines below, explain how the models helped you find the answer.

Because, when I made the model I shaded 3 in 10 and on the 2nd one I shaded in 1 out of 5. And in A I shaded more rectangles than B.

14   Look at the pattern below.

$$16, 19, 22, 25, 28, 31, \underline{34}$$

Part A

Write an expression that can be used to find the next number in the pattern. Use *x* to represent the last number in the pattern.

Expression $\underline{28 + 3 = 31 + 3 = x}$

Part B

Use the expression from Part A to find the next number in the pattern.

Answer $\underline{37}$

Part C

Use the expression from Part A to find the number that would come after 112.

Answer $\underline{115}$

15 Complete the number sentences below to show **three** different ways to complete the calculation in two steps.

$$6 \times 5 \times 3$$

$\boxed{6} \times \boxed{5} = 30$, then $\boxed{30} \times \boxed{3} = \boxed{90}$

$\boxed{3} \times \boxed{6} = 18$, then $\boxed{18} \times \boxed{5} = \boxed{90}$

$\boxed{5} \times \boxed{3} = 15$, then $\boxed{15} \times \boxed{6} = \boxed{90}$

END OF SESSION 1

$$
\begin{array}{r}
\overset{4}{18} \\
+18 \\
+18 \\
+18 \\
+18 \\
\hline
90
\end{array}
$$

PARCC Performance-Based Assessment

Practice Test 1

Session 2

Instructions

Read each question carefully. For each multiple-choice question, fill in the circle for the correct answer. For other types of questions, follow the directions given in the question.

Some questions may ask you to show your work. Be sure to show your work or explain how you found your answer in the space provided.

You may use a ruler to help you answer questions. You may not use a calculator on this test.

16 A company has 8 salespersons. Each salesperson works about 40 hours each week. About how many hours do all the salespeople work in all?

Ⓐ   32

Ⓑ   48

Ⓒ   320

Ⓓ   480

17 A dance class usually has 30 students in it. On Monday, there were 6 students missing from the class and 2 extra students visiting the class. Write the correct symbols in the boxes to complete the number sentence that shows how many students were in the class on Monday. Then complete the calculation.

$$30 \boxed{-} 6 \boxed{+} 2 = \boxed{26}$$

18 There were 17,856 people living in Eastwood in 2009. What is the value of the digit 8 in 17,856?

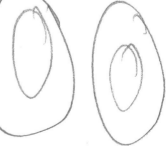

Ⓐ   Eight hundred

Ⓑ   Eight thousand

Ⓒ   Eighty thousand

Ⓓ   Eighty

19 What fraction of the model is shaded?

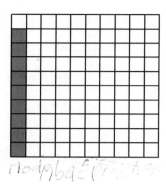

(A) $\dfrac{1}{9}$

(B) $\dfrac{9}{10}$

(C) $\dfrac{9}{91}$

(D) $\dfrac{9}{100}$

20 Which of the following is another way to write quarter past five?

(A) 5:25

(B) 5:30

(C) 5:45

(D) 5:15

21 One Friday, 5 of a hairdresser's customers were male and 15 were female. What fraction of the hairdresser's customers were male? Write your answer in lowest form. Use the diagram below to help find your answer.

Show your work.

Men

Women

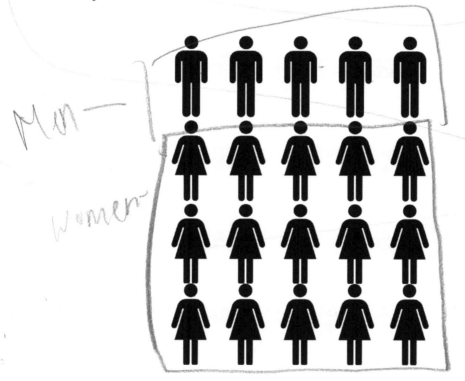

Answer ____ $\frac{5}{15}$ ____ of the customers

22   Which number comes next in the pattern below?

$$4, 8, 16, 32, 64, \underline{128}$$

Show your work.

4+4=8
8+8=16
16+16=32
32+32=64
64+64=128

$$\begin{array}{r} 64 \\ + 64 \\ \hline 128 \end{array}$$

Answer _128_

23 Alana finished school at the time shown on the clock below.

Alana arrived home 15 minutes later. What time did Alana arrive home?

Show your work.

3:30+15=3:45

Answer 3:45

24 A box contains 60 cans of soup. Gerald orders 8 boxes of soup for his store. How many cans of soup does Gerald order?

Show your work.

$$60 \times 8 = 480$$

Answer ___480___ cans of soup

25 Lyn lives 15 miles from her school. Dan lives 3 miles closer than Lyn. How far does Dan live from school?

Show your work.

$$15 - 3 = 12$$

Answer 12 miles

26 The graph shows the number of points four players scored in a basketball game.

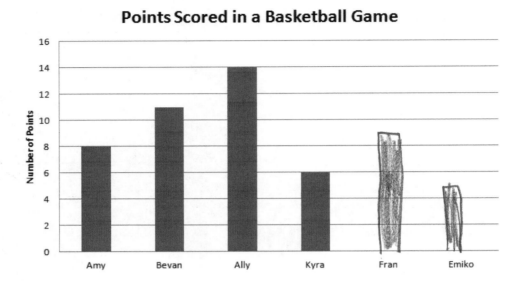

Points Scored in a Basketball Game

Part A

Fran scored 9 points and Emiko scored 5 points. Add two bars to the graph above to show the points scored by Fran and Emiko.

Part B

How many of the players scored more points than Fran?

Answer _____2_____ players

27 Circle all the shapes below that are quadrilaterals.

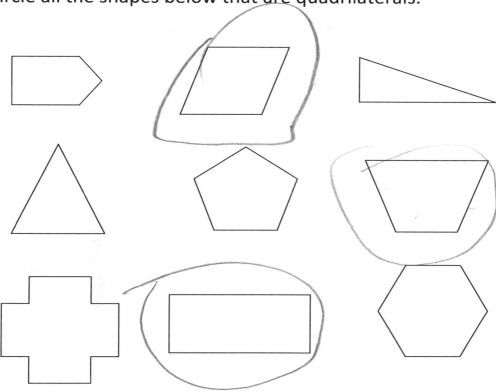

On the lines below, describe the property that is shared by all the shapes you circled.

_____

_____

_____

_____

28   Look at the figure below.

  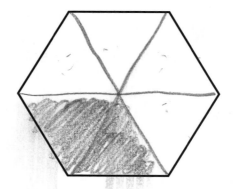

Part A

Divide the shape into 6 equal triangles. Draw lines on the shape above to show your answer.

Part B

Shade 2 of the triangles you divided the shape into. What fraction of the shape is shaded?

Show your work.

Answer $\frac{6}{2}$

29 The top of a rectangular desk is 4 feet long and 3 feet wide.

Part A

What is the area of the top of the desk?

Show your work.

$$4 \times 3 = 12$$

Answer __12__

Part B

What is the perimeter of the top of the desk?

Show your work.

$$4 + 3 = 7$$

Answer __7__

30 Look at the shapes below.

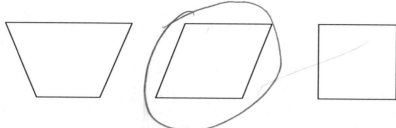

Part A

Circle the rhombus.

Part B

On the lines below, describe **two** ways a rhombus is similar to a square.

1 way is, if you turn a rhombus around it would be a square. A rhombus has 4 corners like a square.

END OF SESSION 2

INTRODUCTION TO THE EOY PRACTICE TEST
For Parents, Teachers, and Tutors

About the End-of-Year Assessment

The End-of-Year Assessment (EOY) is taken after about 90% of the school year is complete. It is designed to allow students to demonstrate that they have the skills and knowledge described in the Common Core State Standards. The EOY Assessment only includes the Type I questions described below.

- **Type I** – these items are straightforward selected response or simple computer-based questions. These items are worth 1 or 2 points.

These items may be simple selected response questions where the one correct answer is selected or selected response questions with 2 or more correct answers. The computer-based questions could involve writing numerical answers, sorting or ordering numbers or items, selecting points on a number line or graph, completing number sentences and equations, or using fraction models. This practice test includes a wide range of formats that mimic the computer-based questions.

The actual test contains 39 Type I items. The practice tests in this book contain 50 Type I items. This will ensure that students have practice with all the types of questions they are likely to encounter on the real test and gain the experience needed to complete questions with a range of new formats.

Taking the Test

Just like the real EOY test, the practice test is divided into two sessions. Each session includes 25 questions. On the real test, students are allowed 2 hours to complete each session. To account for the additional questions, students should be allowed 3 hours for each session of the practice test. Students can complete the two sessions on the same day or on different days, but should have a break between sessions.

Calculators and Tools

Students should be provided with a ruler to use on both sessions of the test. Students are not allowed to use a calculator on any session of the PARCC tests, and so should complete all the practice tests without the use of a calculator.

PARCC End-of-Year Assessment

Practice Test 1

Session 1

Instructions

Read each question carefully. For each multiple-choice question, fill in the circle for the correct answer. For other types of questions, follow the directions given in the question.

You may use a ruler to help you answer questions. You may not use a calculator on this test.

1   Sara walked around the four outside edges of a football fie
    Sara recorded the total distance she walked, what would S
    have determined?

Ⓐ   The area of the football field

Ⓑ   The volume of the football field

Ⓒ   The perimeter of the football field

Ⓓ   The surface area of the football field

2   A piece of note paper has side lengths of 12 centimeters. What is
    the area of the piece of note paper?

Ⓐ   48 square centimeters

Ⓑ   72 square centimeters

Ⓒ   120 square centimeters

Ⓓ   144 square centimeters

3   Leah made 500 cakes of soap to sell at a fair. She sold 182 cakes of soap on Saturday. Then she sold 218 cakes of soap on Sunday. Choose the **two** expressions that can be used to find how many cakes of soap she had left.

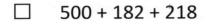

☐   500 + 182 + 218

☐   500 + 182 − 218

▨   500 − 182 − 218

▨   500 − (182 + 218)

☐   500 − (218 − 182)

☐   500 + (218 − 182)

4   Michael drove 1,285 miles during a vacation. How far did Michael drive to the nearest hundred and the nearest ten? Write your answers below.

Nearest hundred: _____ miles

Nearest ten: _____ miles

5   Donna has 18 roses. She wants to put the roses into vases so that each vase has the same number of roses, with no roses left over.

How many roses could Donna put in each vase?

Ⓐ   4

Ⓑ   5

Ⓒ   6

Ⓓ   8

6   Patrick bought 2 packets of 8 pencils for $4 per packet. He also bought 3 packets of 5 crayons for $3 per packet. How much did Patrick spend in all?

Ⓐ $17

Ⓑ $25

Ⓒ $47

Ⓓ $64

7   Look at the shaded figure below.

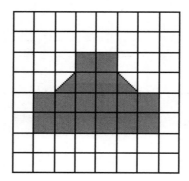

What is the area of the shaded figure?

Ⓐ   17 square units

Ⓑ   16 square units

Ⓒ   18 square units

Ⓓ   24 square units

8   Billy collects pennies and nickels. Billy has 142 pennies and 56 nickels in his coin collection. Which is the best estimate of the total number of coins in Billy's collection?

Ⓐ   150

Ⓑ   180

Ⓒ   200

Ⓓ   250

9   The figure below models the number sentence 6 × 2 = 12.

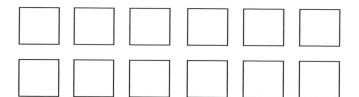

Which number sentence is modeled by the same figure?

Ⓐ   6 ÷ 2 = 3

Ⓑ   36 ÷ 3 = 12

Ⓒ   12 ÷ 6 = 2

Ⓓ   24 ÷ 2 = 12

10   Which numbers make the number sentences below true? Write the numbers in the boxes.

$$18 \times \boxed{} = 18$$

$$18 \times \boxed{} = 0$$

11   The graph shows how far four students travel to school.

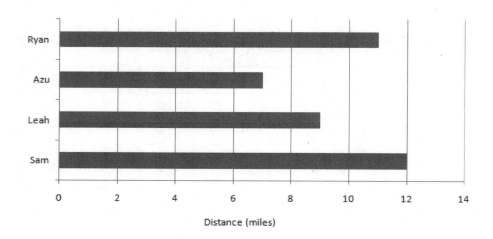

How much farther does Ryan travel than Azu? Write your answer below.

_____ miles

12   What is the total area of the shaded portion of the grid?

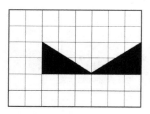

Ⓐ   3 square units

Ⓑ   6 square units

Ⓒ   12 square units

Ⓓ   16 square units

13   A school play was performed on three nights. The table below shows the number of people that saw the school play each night.

Day	Number of People
Friday	225
Saturday	318
Sunday	290

Which number sentence shows the best estimate of the total number of people who saw the school play?

Ⓐ   200 + 300 + 200 = 700

Ⓑ   200 + 300 + 300 = 800

Ⓒ   200 + 400 + 300 = 900

Ⓓ   300 + 400 + 300 = 1,000

14   Aaron has quarters and dimes. Aaron's coins are shown below.

Complete the **two** fractions that show the fraction of coins that are quarters.

$$\frac{\boxed{}}{6} = \frac{\boxed{}}{3}$$

15   Which number sentence represents the array shown below?

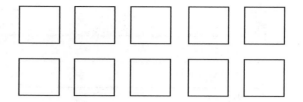

  Ⓐ   5 + 2 = 7

  Ⓑ   5 × 5 = 25

  Ⓒ   5 × 2 = 10

  Ⓓ   5 − 2 = 3

16   Plot the fraction $2\frac{3}{4}$ on the number line below.

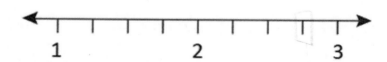

17   The table below shows the different colors of marbles in a bag.

Color	Number of Marbles
Red	5
Green	10
Blue	2
White	3

Match the color with what fraction of the marbles are that color. Draw lines to show the matches.

Red $\dfrac{1}{2}$

Green $\dfrac{1}{10}$

Blue $\dfrac{3}{20}$

White $\dfrac{1}{4}$

18   Leah baked 3 pies. She cut each pie into 8 pieces.

How many pieces of pie does Leah have? Write your answer below.

_____ pieces of pie

19 Sarah needs a screwdriver that is smaller than $\frac{3}{8}$ inch. Which screwdriver sizes are less than $\frac{3}{8}$ inch? Select **all** the correct answers.

☐ $\frac{1}{2}$ inch

☐ $\frac{3}{4}$ inch

☐ $\frac{1}{8}$ inch

☐ $\frac{1}{4}$ inch

☐ $\frac{3}{10}$ inch

☐ $\frac{5}{8}$ inch

20 A dollar bill has a length of 150 mm and a width of 50 mm. Complete the number sentences below to show **two** ways to find the perimeter of the dollar bill, in millimeters.

_____ + _____ + _____ + _____ = _____

2(_____ + _____) = _____

21   Which of these shapes can be divided into two equal triangles by drawing a vertical line down the center?

Ⓐ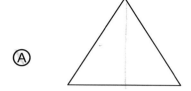

Ⓑ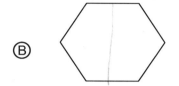

Ⓒ

Ⓓ

22 Kym is going camping. It costs $16 per night for the campsite. Kym plans to stay for 12 nights. How much will the campsite cost for 12 nights?

Ⓐ $82

Ⓑ $144

Ⓒ $168

Ⓓ $192

23 Andrew is selling muffins at a bake sale. The table shows the profit he makes by selling 5, 10, 15, and 20 muffins.

Muffins Sold	Profit Made
5	$15
10	$30
15	$45
20	$60

Based on the table above, how much profit does Andrew make for selling 1 muffin?

Ⓐ $15

Ⓑ $5

Ⓒ $3

Ⓓ $2

24   What is the area of the square below? Write your answer below.

6 cm

_____ cm^2

25   Mrs. Bowen cooked dinner for 24 guests. She cooked 3 courses for each guest. Which equation shows how many courses Mrs. Bowen cooked, *c*?

Ⓐ $24 \times 3 = c$

Ⓑ $24 + 3 = c$

Ⓒ $24 - 3 = c$

Ⓓ $24 \div 3 = c$

END OF SESSION 1

PARCC End-of-Year Assessment

Practice Test 1

Session 2

Instructions

Read each question carefully. For each multiple-choice question, fill in the circle for the correct answer. For other types of questions, follow the directions given in the question.

You may use a ruler to help you answer questions. You may not use a calculator on this test.

26 Which number is 3 more than the product of 4 and 23?

Ⓐ 80

Ⓑ 89

Ⓒ 92

Ⓓ 95

27 The graph below shows the high temperature in Dallas for five days.

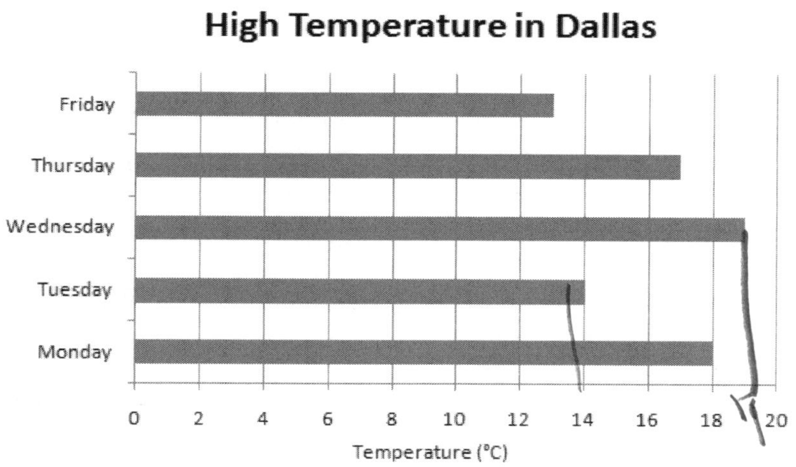
High Temperature in Dallas
Friday
Thursday
Wednesday
Tuesday
Monday
0
2
4
6
8
10
12
14
16
18
20
Temperature (°C)

On which day was the high temperature 5°C less than the day with the highest temperature? Write your answer below.

Tuesday

28 Shade the model below to show a fraction equivalent to $\frac{6}{8}$.

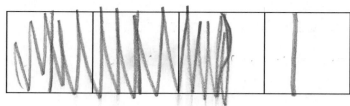

29 Beads are sold in packets of 6 or packets of 8. Liz needs to buy exactly 30 beads. Which set of packets could Liz buy? Select **all** the correct answers.

☐ 5 packets of 6 beads

☐ 5 packets of 8 beads

☐ 1 packet of 8 beads and 2 packets of 6 beads

☐ 2 packets of 8 beads and 2 packets of 6 beads

☐ 1 packet of 8 beads and 3 packets of 6 beads

☐ 3 packets of 8 beads and 1 packet of 6 beads

30 Joy bought a pair of shorts for $11. Then she bought a scarf for $3. Joy had $18 left. Which equation could be used to find how much money Joy had to start with, *m*?

Ⓐ $18 - 11 + 3 = m$

Ⓑ $18 + 11 - 3 = m$

Ⓒ $m + 11 + 3 = 18$

Ⓓ $m - 11 - 3 = 18$

31 The graph shows how long Jody studied each week day.

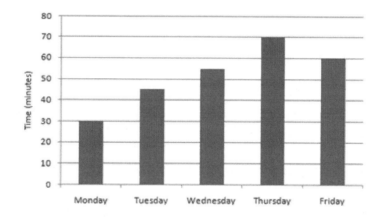

On which day did Jody study for 10 minutes more than the day before?

Ⓐ   Tuesday

Ⓑ   Wednesday

Ⓒ   Thursday

Ⓓ   Friday

32 Davis is making a pictograph to show how many letters three students wrote in a month.

Davis	✉✉✉
Bobby	
Inga	✉✉

Each ✉ means 2 letters.

Bobby wrote 8 letters. How many letter symbols should Davis use to show 8 letters?

Ⓐ 8

Ⓑ 4

Ⓒ 2

Ⓓ 16

33 Ray is slicing apples into 8 slices. Complete the table to show how many apple slices Ray will have if he uses 2, 4, and 5 apples.

Number of Apples	Number of Slices
2	
4	
5	

34 Look at the number pattern below. If the pattern continues, which **two** numbers will come next? Write your answers below.

4, 8, 12, 16, 20, _24_ , _28_

35 Which fraction does the shaded model represent?

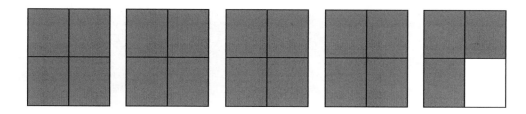

Ⓐ $4\frac{3}{4}$

Ⓑ $4\frac{1}{4}$

Ⓒ $5\frac{3}{4}$

Ⓓ $5\frac{1}{4}$

36   Which fraction model is equivalent to $\frac{1}{2}$?

Ⓐ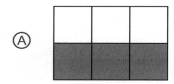

Ⓑ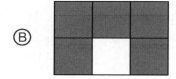

Ⓒ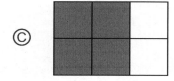

Ⓓ

37   Damien folded the shirts and shorts shown below.

What fraction of the clothes folded were shorts? Write your answer below.

_____

38   David filled the bucket below with water.

About how much water would it take to fill the bucket?

Ⓐ   5 milliliters

Ⓑ   50 milliliters

Ⓒ   5 liters

Ⓓ   50 liters

39   The Walker family drove 182 miles on Saturday. Then they drove 218 miles on Sunday. How many miles did the family travel in all?

Ⓐ   300 miles

Ⓑ   290 miles

Ⓒ   400 miles

Ⓓ   390 miles

40   Margo sorts apples into 1 kilogram bags to sell. Which of these is most likely to be the number of apples in each bag?

Ⓐ   2 apples

Ⓑ   10 apples

Ⓒ   50 apples

Ⓓ   100 apples

41   A bike ride was held to raise money. There were 70 riders and each rider paid $8 to enter. How much money was raised in all?

Ⓐ $506

Ⓑ $560

Ⓒ $568

Ⓓ $580

42 Sam read 39 pages of a novel in one week. He had 165 pages left to read. How many pages does the novel have? Write your answer below.

43 If the numbers below are each rounded to the nearest hundred, which **two** numbers will be rounded up?

- ☒ 10,325
- ☒ 35,682
- ☒ 23,708
- ☒ 71,935
- ☒ 48,540
- ☑ 62,854

44 Leonie has 20 books. She placed an equal number of books on 5 different shelves. There were no books left over.

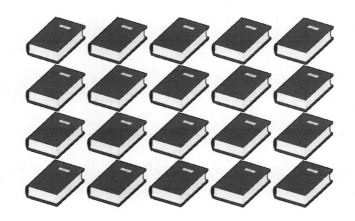

Which number sentence shows how many books Leonie put on each shelf?

Ⓐ   20 + 5 = 25

Ⓑ   20 − 5 = 15

Ⓒ   20 × 5 = 100

Ⓓ   20 ÷ 5 = 4

45 Shade the stars below so that $\frac{1}{3}$ of the stars are shaded.

46   A square garden has side lengths of 8 inches. What is the area of the garden?

Ⓐ   32 square inches

Ⓑ   36 square inches

Ⓒ   48 square inches

Ⓓ   64 square inches

47   Look at the shaded figure below.

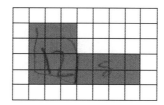

What is the area of the shaded figure?

Ⓐ   20 square units

Ⓑ   22 square units

Ⓒ   26 square units

Ⓓ   28 square units

48 Dannii is training for a bike race. She rode 17 miles on Monday, 19 miles on Tuesday, and 11 miles on Wednesday. Which is the best estimate of how far Dannii rode in all?

Ⓐ   30 miles

Ⓑ   40 miles

Ⓒ   50 miles

Ⓓ   60 miles

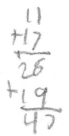

49 Squares and rectangles are quadrilaterals. Which of the shapes below is also a quadrilateral?

Ⓐ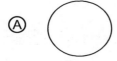

Ⓑ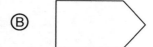

Ⓒ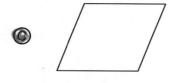

Ⓓ

50 The triangle below has a perimeter of 26 cm.

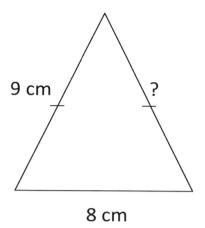

9 cm

?

8 cm

What is the length of the missing side? Write your answer below.

_____9_____ cm

END OF SESSION 2

INTRODUCTION TO THE PBA PRACTICE TEST
For Parents, Teachers, and Tutors

About the Performance-Based Assessment

The Performance-Based Assessment (PBA) is taken after about 75% of the school year is complete. The PBA focuses on applying skills and concepts to solve problems. The emphasis is on completing multi-step problems and advanced tasks. This test is made up of three different types of items, as described below.

- **Type I** – these items are straightforward selected response or simple computer-based questions. These items are worth 1 or 2 points.

- **Type II** – these items are constructed response questions that involve completing more complex tasks and usually require students to show their work, explain their answer, or provide justifications. These items are worth 3 or 4 points.

- **Type III** – these items are complex constructed response questions that involve modeling or applying skills in real-world contexts. These items are worth 3 or 6 points.

The actual test contains 10 Type I items, 4 Type II items, and 3 Type III items. The practice tests in this book contains more questions of each type, especially more Type II and Type III items. This will ensure that students experience all the types of questions they are likely to encounter on the real test and gain the experience needed to complete more rigorous tasks.

Taking the Test

Just like the real EOY test, the practice test is divided into two sessions. Each session includes 15 questions. On the real test, students are allowed 2 hours to complete each session. To account for the additional questions, students should be allowed 4 hours for each session of the practice test. Students can complete the two sessions on the same day or on different days, but should have a break between sessions.

Calculators and Tools

Students should be provided with a ruler to use on both sessions of the test. Students are not allowed to use a calculator on any session of the PARCC tests, and so should complete all the practice tests without the use of a calculator.

PARCC Performance-Based Assessment

Practice Test 2

Session 1

Instructions

Read each question carefully. For each multiple-choice question, fill in the circle for the correct answer. For other types of questions, follow the directions given in the question.

Some questions may ask you to show your work. Be sure to show your work or explain how you found your answer in the space provided.

You may use a ruler to help you answer questions. You may not use a calculator on this test.

1   Which of these shows one way to divide a hexagon into two parts with equal areas?

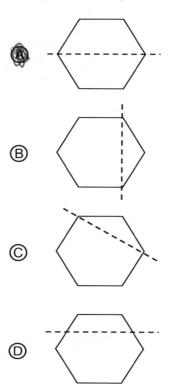

2   There were some people on a bus. After a stop, there were 4 times as many people on the bus. If there were 36 people on the bus after the stop, which equation can be used to find how many people, *p*, were on the bus to start with?

Ⓐ $p \times 4 = 36$

Ⓑ $p \div 4 = 36$

Ⓒ $p + 4 = 36$

Ⓓ $p - 4 = 36$

3   Inga made the design below.

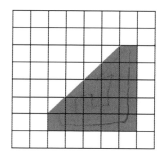

Each square measures 1 square centimeter. What is the area of the shaded part of the design?

  Ⓐ   16 square centimeters

  Ⓑ   17 square centimeters

  Ⓒ   18 square centimeters

  Ⓓ   19 square centimeters

4   Select **all** the statements that describe both a rectangle and a trapezoid.

  ☑   It has four sides.

  ☑   It is a quadrilateral.

  ☐   It has four equal angles.

  ☐   It is a parallelogram.

  ☑   It has two pairs of parallel sides.

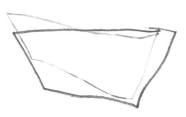

5 What is the best estimate of the mass of a lemon?

Ⓐ   2 grams

Ⓑ   200 grams

Ⓒ   2 kilograms

Ⓓ   200 kilograms

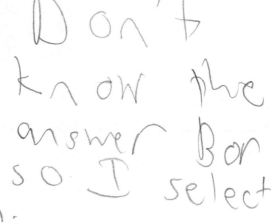

Don't know the answer so I select B or C both.

6 Look at the number pattern below.

48, 42, 36, 30, 24, ...

If the pattern continues, what two numbers will come next?

Ⓐ   22, 20

Ⓑ   30, 36

Ⓒ   20, 16

Ⓓ   18, 12

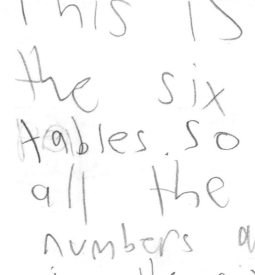

This is the six tables. So all the numbers are in the six table.

7 Rita made the pictograph below to show how many cans each class collected for a food drive.

= 4 cans

How many cans did Miss Lorenzo's class collect? Write your answer below.

_____ cans

8 What is the perimeter of the rectangle below?

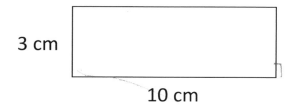

3 cm

10 cm

Ⓐ 13 cm

Ⓑ 30 cm

Ⓒ 26 cm

Ⓓ 60 cm

9   Lei jogs for the same number of minutes every day. The table shows how far she jogs in total after 1, 2, 3, and 4 days. Complete the table to show how many minutes Lei jogs for in total after 5, 6, and 7 days.

Number of Days	Number of Minutes
1	15
2	30
3	45
4	60
5	75
6	90
7	105

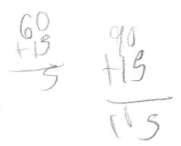

10   The table below shows how many coins of each type Joshua has.

Coin	Number of Coins
Penny	9
Nickel	4
Dime	5
Quarter	2

What fraction of the coins are quarters?

Ⓐ $\frac{1}{2}$

Ⓑ $\frac{1}{4}$

Ⓒ $\frac{1}{10}$

Ⓓ $\frac{1}{20}$

None, it is $\frac{2}{10}$

11   Round 8,782 to the nearest ten and the nearest hundred. Write your answers on the lines below.

Nearest ten <u>8,780</u>

Nearest hundred <u>8,800</u>

On the lines below, explain how you worked out whether to round the number up or down in each case.

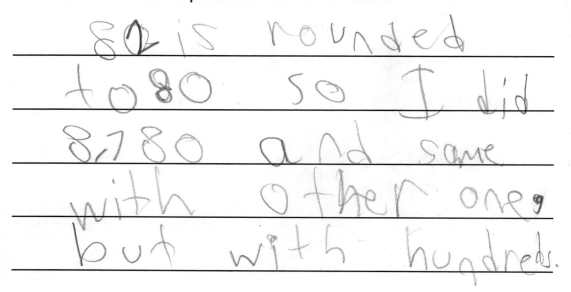

82 is rounded to 80 so I did 8,780 and same with other one but with hundreds.

12 Harris saved $96 in 16 weeks. He saved the same amount of money each week. How much did Harris save each week?

Show your work.

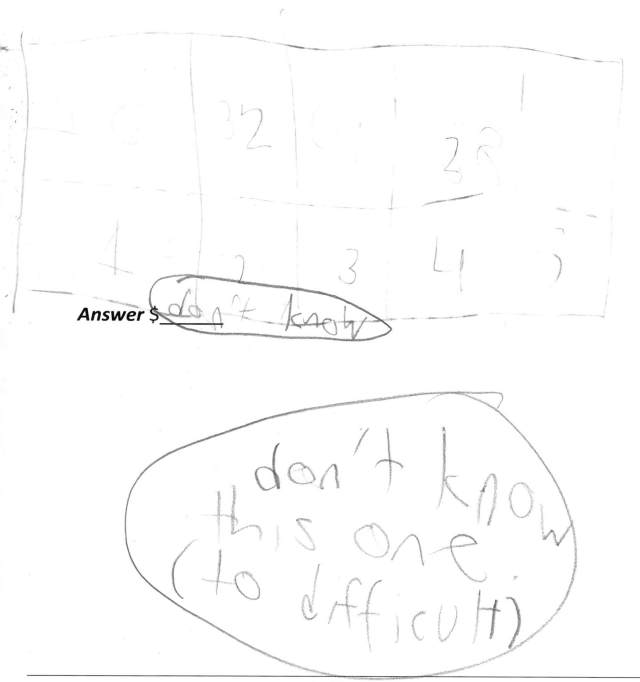

Answer $ don't know

don't know this one. (to difficult)

13 Joy got on a train at 1:35 p.m. Joy got off the train at 3:06 p.m. For how many minutes was Joy on the train?

Show your work.

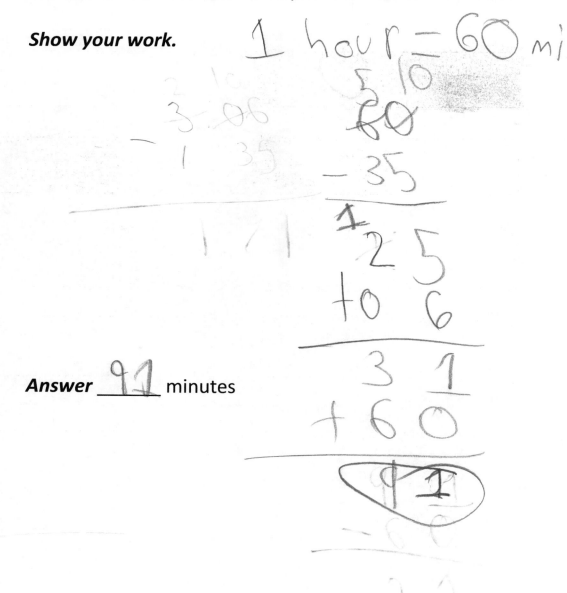

Answer __91__ minutes

14   Part A

Shade the fractions $\frac{1}{2}$ and $\frac{2}{4}$ on the fraction models below.

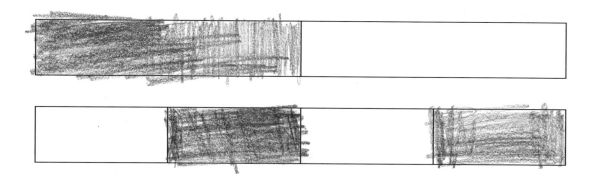

Part B

Shade the fraction model below to show another fraction equivalent to $\frac{1}{2}$ and $\frac{2}{4}$. Write the fraction on the line below.

Answer _____

15   **Part A**

What is the area of the rectangle shown on the grid below?

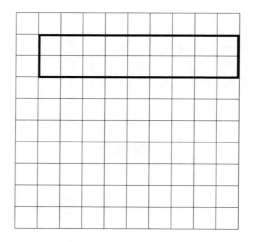

*Answer*_____18_____ square units

Part B

On the grid below, draw a rectangle with the same area but a different perimeter.

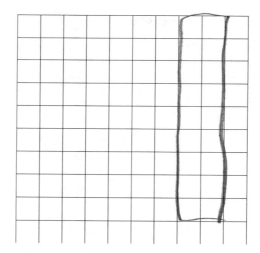

END OF SESSION 1

PARCC Performance-Based Assessment

Practice Test 2

Session 2

Instructions

Read each question carefully. For each multiple-choice question, fill in the circle for the correct answer. For other types of questions, follow the directions given in the question.

Some questions may ask you to show your work. Be sure to show your work or explain how you found your answer in the space provided.

You may use a ruler to help you answer questions. You may not use a calculator on this test.

---

16 Margaret surveyed students about who they would vote for in a class election. Davis made the graph below to show the results.

Davis	☺☺☺☺
Bobby	
Inga	☺☺☺☺☺☺☺

Each ☺ means 2 students.

In the survey, 8 students said they would vote for Bobby. How many symbols should Margaret use to show 8 votes?

Ⓐ   8

Ⓑ   4

Ⓒ   2

Ⓓ   16

17 Kim is 63 inches tall. Chelsea is 4 inches taller than Kim. Vicky is 3 inches shorter than Chelsea. Which expression could be used to find Vicky's height, in inches?

Ⓐ $63 - 4 - 3$

Ⓑ $63 + 4 + 3$

Ⓒ $63 - 4 + 3$

Ⓓ $63 + 4 - 3$

18 Miss Jenkins received wages of $655. She saved $80 of her wages and spent the rest. How much money did Miss Jenkins spend? Write your answer below.

19 Bananas sell for $3 per pound. Stacey buys 9 pounds of bananas. How much would the bananas cost?

- Ⓐ $12
- Ⓑ $27
- Ⓒ $18
- Ⓓ $21

20 A picture frame is 8 inches wide and 5 inches high. What is the perimeter of the frame?

- Ⓐ 26 inches
- Ⓑ 32 inches
- Ⓒ 20 inches
- Ⓓ 40 inches

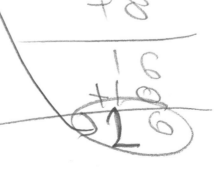

21 **Part A**

Plot the number 48 on the number line below.

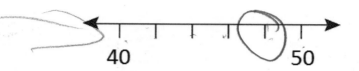

Part B

What is the number 48 rounded to the nearest ten?

Answer _____50_____

On the lines below, explain how the number line helped you round the number.

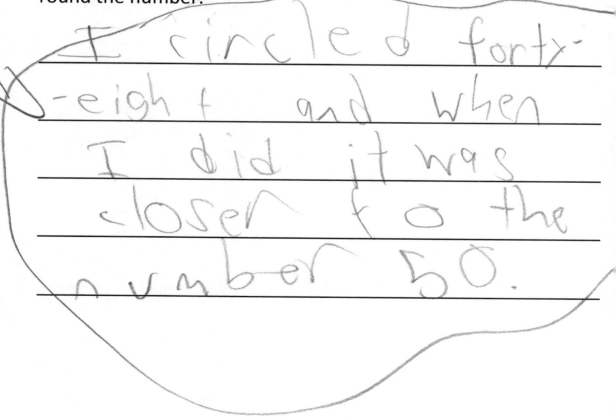

I circled forty-eight and when I did it was closer to the number 50.

22 Apple trees were planted in rows. Each row had the same number of apple trees.

Number of Rows	Number of Apple Trees
4	24
5	30
6	36
7	42

Based on the table, how many apples trees were in each row?

Show your work.

Answer _____ apple trees

23 Mrs. Anderson took out a loan that will take her 60 months to pay off. How many years will it take Mrs. Anderson to pay off the loan?

> 1 year = 12 months

Show your work.

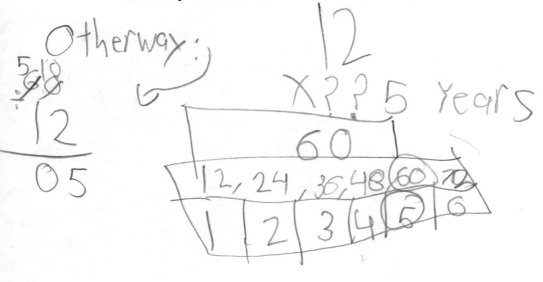

Answer _____5_____ years

24   Georgia made the design below.

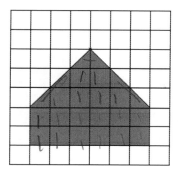

Each square on the grid measures 1 square centimeter. What is the area of the shaded part of the design?

Show your work.

Answer _____ 21 _____ square centimeters

25   The table below shows how many customers a restaurant had on each day of the week.

Day	Number of Customers
Monday	28
Tuesday	21
Wednesday	36
Thursday	32
Friday	45

How many more customers did the restaurant have on Friday than on Monday?

Show your work.

17 more customers on friday than monday.

Answer _____ customers

26 The table below shows Emma's savings over four months.

Month	Amount Saved ($)
Jan	18
Feb	16
Mar	14
Apr	19

Part A

Complete the graph below using the data in the table.

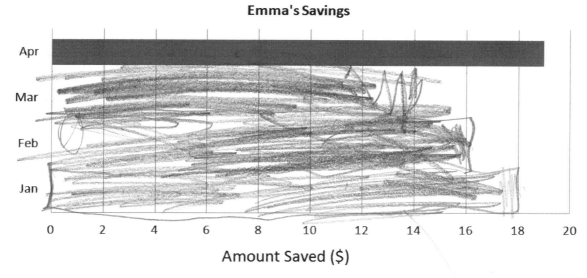

Emma's Savings

Part B

What is the difference between the most and the least she saved each month?

Show your work.

$$19 \; (most)$$
$$- 14 \; (least)$$
$$\boxed{0 \, 5}$$

Answer

27   Look at the number pattern below.

$$7, 10, 13, 16, 19, 22, \underline{25}$$

If the pattern continues, which number will come next?

Answer _____25_____

On the lines below, explain how you found your answer.

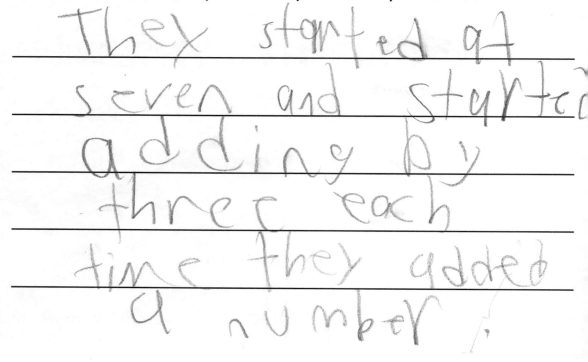

They started at seven and started adding by three each time they added a number.

28   The picture below represents a playground.

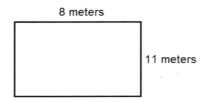

8 meters

11 meters

A fence is being built to go around the edge of the playground. The timber for the fence costs $14 per meter. If enough timber is bought to fit exactly around the edge of the playground, how much will the timber cost?

Show your work.

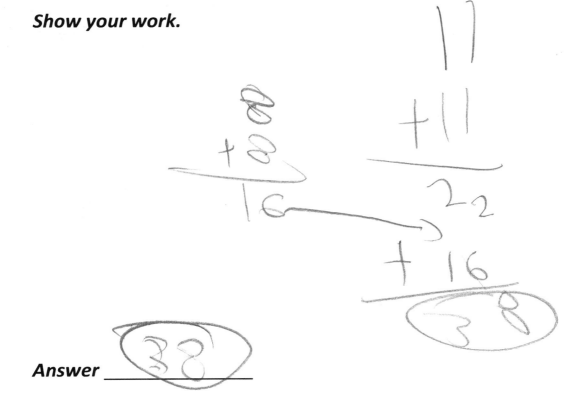

Answer _____

29   During a golf game, Gia scored below par on 3 of the 18 holes.

Part A

Divide the rectangle below into segments and shade the rectangle to show what fraction of the holes Gia scored below par on.

Part B

What fraction of the holes did Gia score below par on? Write your answer in lowest form.

Show your work.

Answer _____

30   What are the two smallest 3-digit numbers that can be made using the digits 1, 6, and 4? Each digit must be used only once in each number.

Answer _____ and _____

On the lines below, explain how you found your answer.

_____

_____

_____

_____

_____

END OF SESSION 2

INTRODUCTION TO THE EOY PRACTICE TEST
For Parents, Teachers, and Tutors

About the End-of-Year Assessment

The End-of-Year Assessment (EOY) is taken after about 90% of the school year is complete. It is designed to allow students to demonstrate that they have the skills and knowledge described in the Common Core State Standards. The EOY Assessment only includes the Type I questions described below.

- **Type I** – these items are straightforward selected response or simple computer-based questions. These items are worth 1 or 2 points.

These items may be simple selected response questions where the one correct answer is selected or selected response questions with 2 or more correct answers. The computer-based questions could involve writing numerical answers, sorting or ordering numbers or items, selecting points on a number line or graph, completing number sentences and equations, or using fraction models. This practice test includes a wide range of formats that mimic the computer-based questions.

The actual test contains 39 Type I items. The practice tests in this book contain 50 Type I items. This will ensure that students have practice with all the types of questions they are likely to encounter on the real test and gain the experience needed to complete questions with a range of new formats.

Taking the Test

Just like the real EOY test, the practice test is divided into two sessions. Each session includes 25 questions. On the real test, students are allowed 2 hours to complete each session. To account for the additional questions, students should be allowed 3 hours for each session of the practice test. Students can complete the two sessions on the same day or on different days, but should have a break between sessions.

Calculators and Tools

Students should be provided with a ruler to use on both sessions of the test. Students are not allowed to use a calculator on any session of the PARCC tests, and so should complete all the practice tests without the use of a calculator.

PARCC End-of-Year Assessment

Practice Test 2

Session 1

Instructions

Read each question carefully. For each multiple-choice question, fill in the circle for the correct answer. For other types of questions, follow the directions given in the question.

You may use a ruler to help you answer questions. You may not use a calculator on this test.

---

1   What fraction of the letter cards below are vowels?

  A E T P S

   Ⓐ $\dfrac{1}{2}$

   Ⓑ $\dfrac{2}{3}$

   Ⓒ $\dfrac{1}{5}$

   Ⓓ $\dfrac{2}{5}$

2   The graph below shows the number of pets four girls have.

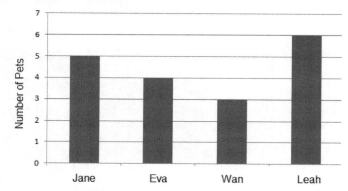

Which two girls have 10 pets in total? Write your answer below.

Eva and _Leah_

3 Rory scored 28 points in a basketball game. Adam scored 4 points less than Rory. Danny scored 6 points more than Adam. How many points did Danny score?

Ⓐ   18

🅑   30

Ⓒ   26

Ⓓ   38

4 Chan had a bag of 27 lollipops. He divided the lollipops evenly between several children.

If there were no lollipops left over, how many lollipops could each child have received? Complete the number sentences below to find the **two** possible answers.

$$\boxed{} \div \boxed{} = \boxed{}$$

$$\boxed{} \div \boxed{} = \boxed{}$$

5   Each square on the grid below is 1 cm wide and 1 cm high.

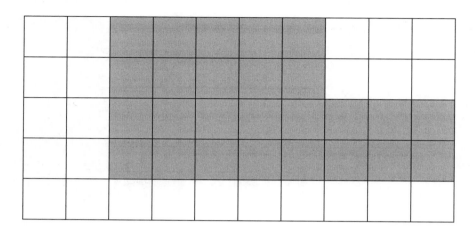

Which **two** expressions could be used to find the area of the shaded figure, in square centimeters?

☐   (5 x 4) + (3 x 2)

☐   (10 x 5) − (5 x 6)

☐   (8 x 2) + (5 x 4)

☐   (8 x 4) − (3 x 2)

☐   (8 x 4) − 3

☐   (10 x 5) − (2 x 6)

6 Ally bought 3 packets of pencils and 2 packets of pens. There were 8 pencils in each packet, and 6 pens in each packet. Which expression could be used to find how many more pencils she bought than pens?

Ⓐ (8 × 6) − (3 × 2)

Ⓑ (8 − 3) × (6 − 2)

Ⓒ (3 × 8) − (2 × 6)

Ⓓ (3 + 8) − (2 + 6)

7 Joy is making gift cards. She puts stars on the front of each card. The table shows how many stars she uses for 3, 5, and 6 cards.

Number of Cards	Number of Stars
3	12
5	20
6	24
8	36

Based on the table, how many stars would Joy need to make 8 cards?

Ⓐ 28

Ⓑ 32

Ⓒ 36

Ⓓ 26

8 Ling scored 82 on a reading test. Mickey scored 63 on the reading test. Which is the best estimate of how many more points Ling scored than Mickey?

Ⓐ   10

Ⓑ   15

Ⓒ   20

Ⓓ   25

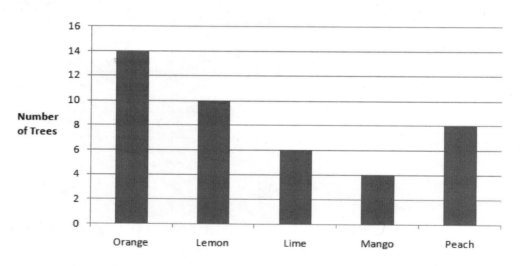

9 The graph below shows the number of different types of trees in an orchard.

How many more orange trees are there than lime and mango trees combined? Write your answer below.

_____4_____ trees

10 A diner has 18 tables. Each table can seat 4 people. The diner also has 8 benches that can each seat 6 people. How many people can the diner seat in all?

   36

ⓑ   120

ⓒ   260

ⓓ   308

11 A rectangle has a length of 6 inches and a height of 5 inches. Complete the number sentences to show **two** ways to find the perimeter of the rectangle, in inches.

_____ + _____ + _____ + _____ = _____

2(_____ + _____) = _____

12   Gregory divided a rectangular piece of cardboard into sections, as shown below.

What fraction of the whole is each section?

Ⓐ $\frac{1}{2}$

Ⓑ $\frac{1}{3}$

Ⓒ $\frac{1}{5}$

Ⓓ $\frac{1}{6}$

13   What is the product of 9 and 8?

Ⓐ   56

Ⓑ   64

Ⓒ   72

Ⓓ   81

14 The grade 3 students at Sam's school are collecting cans for a food drive. The table below shows how many cans each class collected.

Class	Number of Cans
Miss Powell	39
Mr. Sato	22
Mrs. Joshi	26
Mr. Perez	37

Complete the list below by rounding each number to the nearest ten.

Miss Powell   40

Mr. Sato

Mrs. Joshi

Mr. Perez

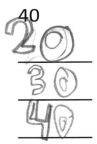

15 Janine bought a packet of muffins. The packet contained 2 chocolate muffins and 6 vanilla muffins.

Complete the **two** fractions that show the fraction of muffins that are chocolate.

$$\frac{\boxed{2}}{8} = \frac{\boxed{?}}{4}$$

16 What fraction does point *J* represent?

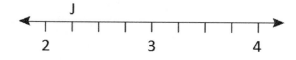

Ⓐ $2\frac{1}{4}$

Ⓑ $2\frac{1}{3}$

Ⓒ $2\frac{1}{5}$

Ⓓ $2\frac{1}{2}$

17 Which number sentence represents the array shown below?

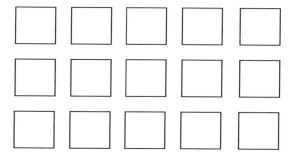

Ⓐ $5 + 3 = 8$

Ⓑ $5 \times 3 = 15$

Ⓒ $15 \times 3 = 45$

Ⓓ $20 - 5 = 15$

18 A pizza has 8 slices. Eriko wants to order enough pizza to have at least 62 slices. What is the least number of pizzas Eriko could order? Write your answer below.

 pizzas

19 Tina completes the calculation below.

$$8 \times 5 = 40$$

Write a division equation that Tina could use to check her calculation.

20 What is the most likely mass of the pumpkin below?

  Ⓐ   5 grams

  Ⓑ   50 grams

  Ⓒ   5 kilograms

  Ⓓ   50 kilograms

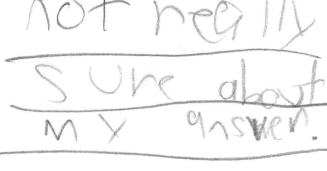

21 Habib measured the length of each wall of his room. A diagram of Habib's room is shown below.

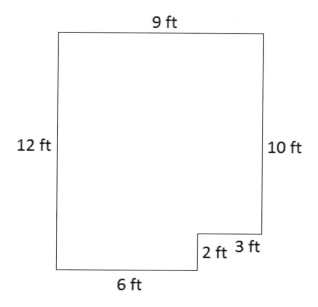

What is the perimeter of Habib's room?

Ⓐ   37 ft

Ⓑ   40 ft

Ⓒ   39 ft

Ⓓ   42 ft

22 Apples are sold in bags. There are the same number of apples in each bag. The table below shows the number of apples in 2, 3, and 4 bags. Complete the table to show the number of apples in 6 bags.

Number of Bags	Number of Apples
2	12
3	18
4	24
6	30

23 Which shape below is a rectangle?

Ⓐ

Ⓑ

Ⓒ

Ⓓ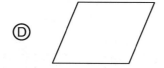

24   Toni has tokens for arcade games.

If Toni counts her tokens in groups of 6, which list shows only numbers she would count?

Ⓐ   6, 8, 10, 12

Ⓑ   6, 10, 16, 20

Ⓒ   12, 18, 24, 30

Ⓓ   12, 16, 20, 24

25   Which of these is another way of expressing 6×14?

Ⓐ $(6 \times 10) + (6 \times 4)$

Ⓑ $(6 \times 1) + (6 \times 4)$

Ⓒ $(6 \times 10) + 4$

Ⓓ $(6 \times 4) + 10$

END OF SESSION 1

PARCC End-of-Year Assessment

Practice Test 2

Session 2

Instructions

Read each question carefully. For each multiple-choice question, fill in the circle for the correct answer. For other types of questions, follow the directions given in the question.

You may use a ruler to help you answer questions. You may not use a calculator on this test.

26 There are 36 students in a class. The teacher needs to divide the students in the class into teams. Each team must have the same number of students in it. There cannot be any students left over. Which of the following could describe the teams? Select **all** the correct answers.

- ☒ 7 teams of 4 students

- ☑ 9 teams of 4 students

- ☒ 6 teams of 5 students

- ☑ 6 teams of 6 students

- ☒ 8 teams of 4 students

- ☒ 9 teams of 3 students

27 The pictograph shows the emails Sammy sent each week day.

Monday	✉✉✉
Tuesday	✉✉
Wednesday	✉✉✉✉
Thursday	✉✉✉
Friday	✉✉✉✉✉✉

Each ✉ means 2 emails.

How many emails did Sammy send on Wednesday? Write your answer below.

 emails

28   What time is shown on the clock below?

   Ⓐ   6:30

   Ⓑ   7:30

   Ⓒ   6:15

   Ⓓ   6:45

29   A square garden has side lengths of 8 inches. Jackie makes a rectangular garden with the same area as the square garden. Whic of these could be the dimensions of the rectangular garden?

   Ⓐ   10 inches by 6 inches

   Ⓑ   7 inches by 9 inches

   Ⓒ   8 inches by 12 inches

   Ⓓ   16 inches by 4 inches

30 Naomi is making a pictograph to show how many fruit trees there are in her yard. The pictograph she has made so far is shown below.

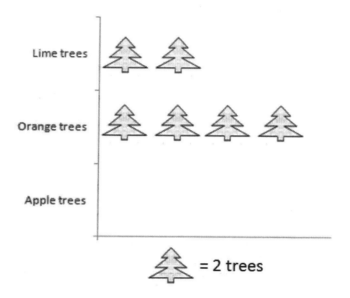

There are 6 apple trees in Naomi's yard. How many tree symbols should Naomi use to show 6 apple trees?

Ⓐ   3

Ⓑ   2

Ⓒ   12

Ⓓ   6

31 Chloe has a 2,000 gram bag of flour. She divides it into smaller bags of 250 grams each. How many smaller bags does she divide the flour into?

Ⓐ 4

Ⓑ 5

Ⓒ 8

Ⓓ 10

32 Shade the model below to show a fraction equivalent to $\frac{1}{4}$.

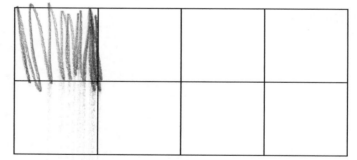

33 A school has 7 school buses. Each bus can seat 48 students. What is the total number of students the buses can seat? Write your answer below.

_____ students

34   What is the length of the piece of lace shown below?

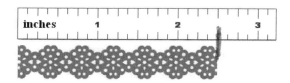

Ⓐ   2 inches

Ⓑ $2\frac{1}{2}$ inches

Ⓒ $2\frac{1}{3}$ inches

Ⓓ $2\frac{1}{4}$ inches

35   Ribbon costs $4 per yard. Allie has $24 to spend on ribbon. Which equation could be used to find how many yards of ribbon, *y*, she can buy?

Ⓐ $4 \times 24 = y$

Ⓑ $4 \div 24 = y$

Ⓒ $4 \times y = 24$

Ⓓ $4 \div y = 24$

36   Reggie's train leaves at the time shown on the clock below.

1:15

What time does Reggie's train leave?

Ⓐ   3:00

Ⓑ   1:15

Ⓒ   1:10

Ⓓ   3:05

37   What do the shaded models below show?

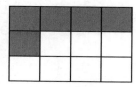 

Ⓐ $\dfrac{5}{12} > \dfrac{1}{3}$

Ⓑ $\dfrac{5}{12} = \dfrac{1}{3}$

Ⓒ $\dfrac{5}{12} < \dfrac{4}{12}$

Ⓓ $\dfrac{5}{7} < \dfrac{2}{3}$

38 Which number sentence represents the array shown below?

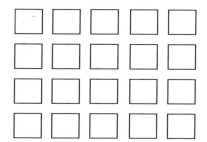

   Ⓐ $5 + 4 = 9$

   Ⓑ $5 \times 5 = 25$

   Ⓒ $5 \times 4 = 20$

   Ⓓ $5 - 4 = 1$

39 Lydia eats 2 pieces of fruit every day. Complete the table to show how many pieces of fruit Lydia eats in 5, 7, and 14 days.

Number of Days	Number of Pieces of Fruit
5	10
7	14
14	28

40   Melinda buys bagels in packets of 4.

If Melinda counts the bagels in groups of 4, which numbers would she count? Circle **all** the numbers she would count.

(18)   20   (22)   (26)

(30)   32   (42)   44

41   Tim scored 21 points in a basketball game. Emmett scored 7 more points than Tim. Which method can be used to find how many points Tim and Emmett scored together?

Ⓐ   Add 21 and 7

🅱   Add 21 to the sum of 21 and 7

Ⓒ   Add 21 to the difference of 21 and 7

Ⓓ   Subtract 7 from 21

42   Place the fractions below in order from smallest to greatest.
Write the numbers 1, 2, 3, and 4 on the lines to show the order.

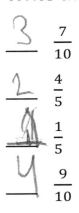

_3_ $\dfrac{7}{10}$

_2_ $\dfrac{4}{5}$

_1_ $\dfrac{1}{5}$

_4_ $\dfrac{9}{10}$

43   There are 28 students at basketball training. The coach needs to divide the students into groups. Each group must have the same number of students in it. There cannot be any students left over. Which of the following could describe the groups?

Ⓐ   7 groups of 4 students

Ⓑ   8 groups of 3 students

Ⓒ   6 groups of 4 students

Ⓓ   10 groups of 3 students

44 Annie collects baseball cards. She has 22 cards in her collection. She gave her sister 2 baseball cards. Then Annie bought 4 new baseball cards. Which expression can be used to find the number of baseball cards Annie has now?

Ⓐ   22 + 2 + 4

Ⓑ   22 + 2 − 4

Ⓒ   22 − 2 + 4

Ⓓ   22 − 2 − 4

45 Nate plotted a fraction on the number line below.

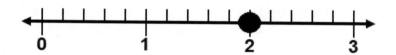

Which fractions could Nate have been plotting? Select **all** the correct answers.

☐ $\frac{1}{2}$

☑ $\frac{2}{2}$

☐ $\frac{4}{2}$

☐ $\frac{8}{4}$

☐ $\frac{4}{8}$

46 The pictograph below shows how long Tamika spent at the computer each week day.

Monday	🖥🖥🖥🖥
Tuesday	🖥🖥🖥🖥🖥🖥
Wednesday	🖥🖥🖥🖥🖥
Thursday	🖥🖥🖥
Friday	🖥🖥

Each 🖥 means 10 minutes.

How long did Tamika spend at the computer on Wednesday?

Ⓐ   15 minutes

Ⓑ   60 minutes

Ⓒ   5 minutes

Ⓓ   50 minutes

47 A recipe for meatballs calls for $\frac{1}{2}$ teaspoon of cumin. Complete the fractions below to show **two** fractions equivalent to $\frac{1}{2}$.

$$\frac{1}{6} \quad \text{and} \quad \frac{6}{?}$$

48   Dean drew these shapes.

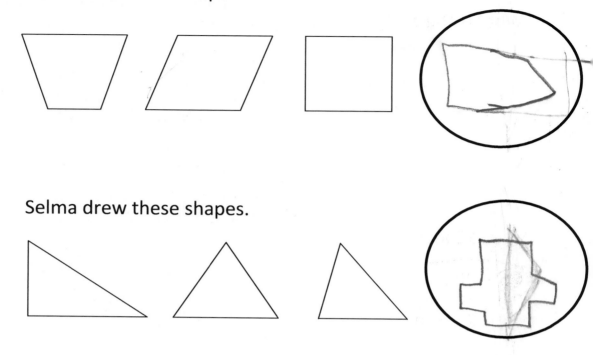

Selma drew these shapes.

Add **one** of the shapes below to Dean's shapes and **one** of the shapes below to Selma's shapes. Draw each shape in the empty circle.

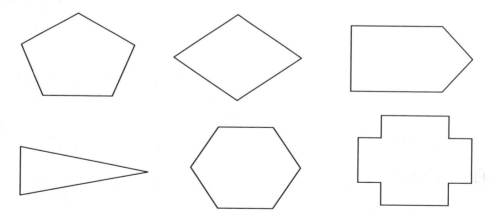

49   A piece of square note paper has side lengths of 5 inches each. What is the perimeter of the note paper?

Ⓐ   10 inches

Ⓑ   20 inches

Ⓒ   25 inches

Ⓓ   30 inches

50   Which measurement is the most likely mass of the apple?

Ⓐ   1 gram

Ⓑ   10 grams

Ⓒ   100 grams

Ⓓ   1,000 grams

END OF SESSION 2

ANSWER KEY

Common Core State Standards

The state of New Jersey has adopted the Common Core State Standards. Student learning throughout the year is based on these standards, and all the questions on the state tests assess these standards. Just like the real PARCC assessments, the questions in this book test whether students have the knowledge and skills described in the Common Core State Standards.

Assessing Skills and Knowledge

The skills listed in the Common Core State Standards are divided into five topics, or clusters. These are:

- Operations and Algebraic Thinking
- Number and Operations in Base Ten
- Number and Operations – Fractions
- Measurement and Data
- Geometry

The answer key identifies the topic for each question. Use the topics listed to identify general areas of strength and weakness. Then target revision and instruction accordingly.

The answer key also identifies the specific math skill that each question is testing. Use the skills listed to identify skills that the student is lacking. Then target revision and instruction accordingly.

Scoring Constructed Response Questions

This practice test book includes constructed response questions, where students provide a written answer to a question or complete a task. These questions are often scored based on the final answer given as well as the work shown. When asked to show work, students may show calculations, use diagrams, or explain their thinking or process in words. Any form of work that shows the student's understanding can be accepted. Other questions are scored based on tasks completed, explanations given, or justifications given. Answers are provided for these questions, as well as guidance on how to score the questions.

PARCC Performance-Based Assessment, Practice Test 1, Session 1

Question	Answer	Topic	Common Core Skill
1	18, 30, 36, 42	Operations/Algebraic Thinking	Interpret products of whole numbers, e.g., interpret 5×7 as the total number of objects in 5 groups of 7 objects each.
2	Wednesday	Measurement & Data	Solve one- and two-step "how many more" and "how many less" problems using information presented in scaled bar graphs.
3	$\frac{4}{1}$ and $\frac{12}{3}$	Number & Operations-Fractions	Express whole numbers as fractions, and recognize fractions that are equivalent to whole numbers.
4	B	Measurement & Data	Draw a scaled picture graph to represent a data set with several categories.
5	B	Operations/Algebraic Thinking	Solve two-step word problems using the four operations.
6	C	Operations/Algebraic Thinking	Represent problems using equations with a letter standing for the unknown quantity.
7	25,600	Number & Operations in Base Ten	Use place value understanding to round whole numbers to the nearest 10 or 100.
8	1,500 + 1,600 + 1,200 = 4,300	Operations/Algebraic Thinking	Assess the reasonableness of answers using mental computation and estimation strategies including rounding.
9	A	Number & Operations in Base Ten	Fluently add and subtract within 1000 using strategies and algorithms based on place value, properties of operations, and/or the relationship between addition and subtraction.
10	Point at $1\frac{1}{4}$	Number & Operations-Fractions	Understand a fraction as a number on the number line; represent fractions on a number line diagram.
11	See Below	Number & Operations in Base Ten	Use place value understanding to round whole numbers to the nearest 10 or 100.
12	See Below	Number & Operations-Fractions	Understand a fraction $1/b$ as the quantity formed by 1 part when a whole is partitioned into b equal parts.
13	See Below	Number & Operations-Fractions	Compare two fractions with the same numerator or the same denominator by reasoning about their size. Record the results of comparisons with the symbols >, =, or <, and justify the conclusions, e.g., by using a visual fraction model.
14	See Below	Operations/Algebraic Thinking	Identify arithmetic patterns, and explain them using properties of operations.
15	See Below	Operations/Algebraic Thinking	Apply properties of operations as strategies to multiply and divide.

Q11.
110, 90, 280, 980, 860, 200, 40, 770

Explanation
The student should provide an explanation that refers to considering the number in the ones place. The answer should include that the number is rounded down if the number is less than 5 and rounded up if the number is 5 or higher.

Scoring Information
Give a total score out of 4.
Give a score of 0.25 for each number correctly rounded.
Give a score out of 2 for the explanation.

Q12.
Answer
$\frac{5}{19}$

Work
The work should show winning 5 games out of a total of 5 + 14 = 19 games.

Scoring Information
Give a total score out of 3.
Give a score of 1 for the correct answer.
Give a score out of 2 for the working.

Q13.
The two models should have shaded 3 of the 10 segments and 2 of the 10 segments.
The > symbol should be placed in the empty box.

Explanation
The student may explain how shading the models allows the two fractions to be compared by seeing how many parts of 10 each fraction is. The student may explain how you can compare the fractions as parts of the same whole.

Scoring Information
Give a total score out of 4.
Give a score of 1 for each correct shading.
Give a score of 1 for the correct symbol.
Give a score out of 2 for the explanation.

Q14.
Part A
Expression
$x + 3$

Part B
Answer
34

Part C
Answer
115

Scoring Information
Give a total score out of 3.
Give a score of 1 for the correct expression in Part A.
Give a score of 1 for the correct answer in Part B.
Give a score of 1 for the correct answer in Part C.

Q15.
$6 \times 5 = 30$, then $30 \times 3 = 90$ OR $5 \times 6 = 30$, then $30 \times 3 = 90$
$6 \times 3 = 18$, then $18 \times 5 = 90$ OR $3 \times 6 = 18$, then $18 \times 5 = 90$
$5 \times 3 = 15$, then $15 \times 6 = 90$ OR $3 \times 5 = 15$, then $15 \times 6 = 90$

Scoring Information
Give a total score out of 3.
Give a score of 1 for each correct number sentence.

PARCC Performance-Based Assessment, Practice Test 1, Session 2

Question	Answer	Topic	Common Core Skill
16	C	Number & Operations in Base Ten	Multiply one-digit whole numbers by multiples of 10 in the range 10–90 using strategies based on place value and properties of operations.
17	30 – 6 + 2 = 26	Operations/Algebraic Thinking	Solve two-step word problems using the four operations. Represent these problems using equations with a letter standing for the unknown quantity.
18	A	Number & Operations in Base Ten	Use place value understanding.
19	D	Number & Operations-Fractions	Understand a fraction 1/b as the quantity formed by 1 part when a whole is partitioned into b equal parts.
20	D	Measurement & Data	Tell and write time to the nearest minute and measure time intervals in minutes.
21	See Below	Number & Operations-Fractions	Understand a fraction 1/b as the quantity formed by 1 part when a whole is partitioned into b equal parts; understand a fraction a/b as the quantity formed by a parts of size 1/b.
22	See Below	Operations/Algebraic Thinking	Identify arithmetic patterns, and explain them using properties of operations.
23	See Below	Measurement & Data	Tell and write time to the nearest minute and measure time intervals in minutes. Solve word problems involving addition and subtraction of time intervals in minutes.
24	See Below	Number & Operations in Base Ten	Multiply one-digit whole numbers by multiples of 10 in the range 10–90 using strategies based on place value and properties of operations.
25	See Below	Number & Operations in Base Ten	Fluently add and subtract within 1000 using strategies and algorithms based on place value, properties of operations, and/or the relationship between addition and subtraction.
26	See Below	Measurement & Data	Draw a scaled bar graph to represent a data set with several categories. Solve one- and two-step "how many more" and "how many less" problems using information presented in scaled bar graphs.
27	See Below	Geometry	Understand that shapes in different categories (e.g., rhombuses, rectangles, and others) may share attributes (e.g., having four sides), and that the shared attributes can define a larger category (e.g., quadrilaterals).
28	See Below	Geometry	Partition shapes into parts with equal areas. Express the area of each part as a unit fraction of the whole.
29	See Below	Measurement & Data	Solve real world and mathematical problems involving areas and perimeters of rectangles.
30	See Below	Geometry	Understand that shapes in different categories may share attributes, and that the shared attributes can define a larger category.

Q21.
Answer
$\frac{1}{4}$ of the customers

Work
The work should use the diagram to show that 1 out of 4 customers were male.

Scoring Information
Give a total score out of 3.
Give a score of 2 for the correct answer. Give a score of 1 if the fraction $\frac{5}{20}$ is given.
Give a score out of 1 for the working.

Q22.
Answer
128

Work
The work should show that the student understands that each number in the pattern is twice the one before it.

Scoring Information
Give a total score out of 3.
Give a score of 1 for the correct answer.
Give a score out of 2 for the working.

Q23.
Answer
3:45

Work
The work should show that the clock shows 3:30, and then add 15 minutes to this time.

Scoring Information
Give a total score out of 3.
Give a score of 1 for the correct answer.
Give a score out of 2 for the working.

Q24.
Answer
480 cans of soup

Work
The work should show the calculation of 60 × 8 = 480. The work may show the calculation of 6 × 8 = 48, and then the addition of a zero to the end of the number to give 480.

Scoring Information
Give a total score out of 3.
Give a score of 1 for the correct answer.
Give a score out of 2 for the working.

Q25.
Answer
12 miles

Work
The work should show the calculation of 15 − 3 = 12.

Scoring Information
Give a total score out of 3.
Give a score of 1 for the correct answer.
Give a score out of 2 for the working.

Q26.
Part A
The student should add a bar to 9 for Fran and a bar to 5 for Emiko.

Part B
Answer
2 players

Scoring Information
Give a total score out of 6.
Give a score out of 2 for each bar added in Part A.
Give a score of 2 for the correct answer in Part B.
Give a score of 1 for Part B if the student lists the players instead of giving the number of players.

Q27.
The rhombus, the trapezoid, and the rectangle should be circled.

Explanation
The property identified could be that all the shapes have four sides or that all the shapes have four angles.

Scoring Information
Give a total score out of 4.
Give a score of 2 if the three shapes are correctly circled.
Give a score of 1 if only 1 or 2 of the shapes are correctly circled, or if additional shapes are also circled.
Give a score out of 2 for the explanation.

Q28.
Part A
The student should divide the hexagon into 6 equal triangles, as shown below.

Part B
Answer
$\frac{1}{3}$ or $\frac{2}{6}$

Scoring Information
Give a total score out of 3.
Give a score of 1 for a correct division into 6 triangles in Part A.
Give a score of 1 for the correct answer in Part B.
Give a score out of 1 for the working in Part B.

Q29.
Part A
Answer
12 square feet

Work
The work could show the calculation 4 × 3 = 12, or could use a diagram of a 4 by 3 rectangle.

Part B
Answer
14 feet

Work
The work should show the calculation 4 + 4 + 3 + 3 = 14 or (2 × 4) + (2 × 3) = 14.

Scoring Information
Give a total score out of 4.
Give a score of 1 for the correct answer to Part A.
Give a score out of 1 for the working in Part A.
Give a score of 1 for the correct answer to Part B.
Give a score out of 1 for the working in Part B.

Q30.
Part A
The rhombus in the center should be circled.

Part B
Answers may describe any two of the following similarities:
- They both have 4 sides or 4 equal sides.
- They both have 4 angles.
- They both have congruent or equal sides.
- They both have parallel sides.

Scoring Information
Give a total score out of 3.
Give a score of 1 for the correct shape circled.
Give a score of 1 for each similarity correctly described.

PARCC End-Of-Year Assessment, Practice Test 1, Session 1

Question	Answer	Topic	Common Core Skill
1	C	Measurement & Data	Recognize perimeter as an attribute of plane figures and distinguish between linear and area measures.
2	D	Measurement & Data	Multiply side lengths to find areas of rectangles with whole-number side lengths in the context of solving real world and mathematical problems.
3	3rd and 4th	Operations/Algebraic Thinking	Solve two-step word problems using the four operations.
4	1,300 1,290	Number & Operations in Base Ten	Use place value understanding to round whole numbers to the nearest 10 or 100.
5	C	Operations/Algebraic Thinking	Interpret whole-number quotients of whole numbers, e.g., interpret $56 \div 8$ as the number of objects in each share when 56 objects are partitioned equally into 8 shares.
6	A	Operations/Algebraic Thinking	Solve two-step word problems using the four operations.
7	A	Measurement & Data	Recognize area as an attribute of plane figures and understand concepts of area measurement, including that a plane figure which can be covered without gaps or overlaps by n unit squares is said to have an area of n square units.
8	C	Operations/Algebraic Thinking	Assess the reasonableness of answers using mental computation and estimation strategies including rounding.
9	C	Operations/Algebraic Thinking	Interpret products of whole numbers and whole-number quotients of whole numbers.
10	1, 0	Operations/Algebraic Thinking	Determine the unknown whole number in a multiplication or division equation relating three whole numbers.
11	4 miles	Measurement & Data	Solve one- and two-step "how many more" and "how many less" problems using information presented in scaled bar graphs.
12	B	Measurement & Data	Recognize area as an attribute of plane figures and understand concepts of area measurement, including that a plane figure which can be covered without gaps or overlaps by n unit squares is said to have an area of n square units.
13	B	Number & Operations in Base Ten	Use place value understanding to round whole numbers to the nearest 10 or 100.
14	$\frac{2}{6}$ and $\frac{1}{3}$	Number & Operations-Fractions	Recognize and generate simple equivalent fractions. Explain why the fractions are equivalent, e.g., by using a visual fraction model.
15	C	Operations/Algebraic Thinking	Interpret products of whole numbers, e.g., interpret 5 × 7 as the total number of objects in 5 groups of 7 objects each.
16	Point at $2\frac{3}{4}$	Number & Operations-Fractions	Understand a fraction as a number on the number line; represent fractions on a number line diagram.

17	Red $\frac{1}{4}$ Green $\frac{1}{2}$ Blue $\frac{1}{10}$ White $\frac{3}{20}$	Number & Operations-Fractions	Understand a fraction 1/b as the quantity formed by 1 part when a whole is partitioned into b equal parts; understand a fraction a/b as the quantity formed by a parts of size 1/b.
18	24 pieces of pie	Operations/Algebraic Thinking	Use multiplication and division within 100 to solve word problems in situations involving equal groups.
19	$\frac{1}{8}, \frac{1}{4}, \frac{3}{10}$	Number & Operations-Fractions	Compare two fractions with the same numerator or the same denominator by reasoning about their size.
20	150 + 150 + 50 + 50 = 400 2(150 + 50) = 400	Measurement & Data	Solve real world and mathematical problems involving perimeters of polygons.
21	A	Geometry	Partition shapes into parts with equal areas.
22	D	Operations/Algebraic Thinking	Apply properties of operations as strategies to multiply and divide.
23	C	Operations/Algebraic Thinking	Identify arithmetic patterns, and explain them using properties of operations.
24	36 cm^2	Measurement & Data	Multiply side lengths to find areas of rectangles with whole-number side lengths in the context of solving real world and mathematical problems.
25	A	Operations/Algebraic Thinking	Represent problems using equations with a letter standing for the unknown quantity.

PARCC End-Of-Year Assessment, Practice Test 1, Session 2

Question	Answer	Topic	Common Core Skill
26	D	Operations/Algebraic Thinking	Solve two-step word problems using the four operations.
27	Tuesday	Measurement & Data	Solve one- and two-step "how many more" and "how many less" problems using information presented in scaled bar graphs.
28	Any 3 of the 4 squares shaded	Number & Operations-Fractions	Recognize and generate simple equivalent fractions. Explain why the fractions are equivalent, e.g., by using a visual fraction model.
29	1st and 6th	Operations/Algebraic Thinking	Use multiplication and division within 100 to solve word problems in situations involving equal groups, arrays, and measurement quantities.
30	D	Operations/Algebraic Thinking	Represent problems using equations with a letter standing for the unknown quantity.
31	B	Measurement & Data	Solve one- and two-step "how many more" and "how many less" problems using information presented in scaled bar graphs.
32	B	Measurement & Data	Draw a scaled picture graph to represent a data set with several categories.
33	16, 32, 40	Operations/Algebraic Thinking	Use multiplication and division within 100 to solve word problems in situations involving equal groups, arrays, and measurement quantities.
34	24, 28	Operations/Algebraic Thinking	Identify arithmetic patterns, and explain them using properties of operations.
35	A	Number & Operations-Fractions	Understand a fraction $1/b$ as the quantity formed by 1 part when a whole is partitioned into b equal parts; understand a fraction a/b as the quantity formed by a parts of size $1/b$.
36	A	Number & Operations-Fractions	Recognize and generate simple equivalent fractions. Explain why the fractions are equivalent, e.g., by using a visual fraction model.
37	$\frac{2}{5}$	Number & Operations-Fractions	Understand a fraction $1/b$ as the quantity formed by 1 part when a whole is partitioned into b equal parts.
38	C	Measurement & Data	Measure and estimate liquid volumes.
39	C	Number & Operations in Base Ten	Fluently add and subtract within 1000 using strategies and algorithms.
40	B	Measurement & Data	Measure and estimate liquid volumes and masses of objects using standard units of grams (g), kilograms (kg), and liters (l). Add, subtract, multiply, or divide to solve one-step word problems involving masses or volumes that are given in the same units.
41	B	Number & Operations in Base Ten	Multiply one-digit whole numbers by multiples of 10 in the range 10–90 using strategies based on place value and properties of operations.
42	204	Number & Operations in Base Ten	Fluently add and subtract within 1000 using strategies and algorithms based on place value, properties of operations, and/or the relationship between addition and subtraction.

43	35,682 62,854	Number & Operations in Base Ten	Use place value understanding to round whole numbers to the nearest 10 or 100.
44	D	Operations/Algebraic Thinking	Interpret whole-number quotients of whole numbers, e.g., interpret 56 ÷ 8 as the number of objects in each share when 56 objects are partitioned equally into 8 shares, or as a number of shares when 56 objects are partitioned into equal shares of 8 objects each.
45	Any 3 of the 9 stars shaded	Number & Operations-Fractions	Understand a fraction $1/b$ as the quantity formed by 1 part when a whole is partitioned into b equal parts; understand a fraction a/b as the quantity formed by a parts of size $1/b$.
46	D	Measurement & Data	Multiply side lengths to find areas of rectangles with whole-number side lengths in the context of solving real world and mathematical problems.
47	A	Measurement & Data	Find areas of rectilinear figures by decomposing them into non-overlapping rectangles and adding the areas of the non-overlapping parts.
48	C	Operations/Algebraic Thinking	Assess the reasonableness of answers using mental computation and estimation strategies including rounding.
49	C	Geometry	Understand that shapes in different categories (e.g., rhombuses, rectangles, and others) may share attributes (e.g., having four sides), and that the shared attributes can define a larger category (e.g., quadrilaterals). Recognize rhombuses, rectangles, and squares as examples of quadrilaterals.
50	9 cm	Measurement & Data	Solve real world and mathematical problems involving perimeters of polygons, including finding an unknown side length.

PARCC Performance-Based Assessment, Practice Test 2, Session 1

Question	Answer	Topic	Common Core Skill
1	A	Geometry	Partition shapes into parts with equal areas. Express the area of each part as a unit fraction of the whole.
2	A	Operations/Algebraic Thinking	Understand division as an unknown-factor problem.
3	B	Measurement & Data	Recognize area as an attribute of plane figures and understand concepts of area measurement, including that a plane figure which can be covered without gaps or overlaps by n unit squares is said to have an area of n square units.
4	1st and 2nd	Geometry	Understand that shapes in different categories may share attribute, and that the shared attributes can define a larger category (e.g., quadrilaterals).
5	B	Measurement & Data	Measure and estimate masses of objects.
6	D	Operations/Algebraic Thinking	Identify arithmetic patterns, and explain them using properties of operations.
7	16 cans	Measurement & Data	Draw a scaled picture graph to represent a data set with several categories.
8	C	Measurement & Data	Solve real world and mathematical problems involving perimeters of polygons, including finding the perimeter given the side lengths.
9	75, 90, 105	Operations/Algebraic Thinking	Identify arithmetic patterns, and explain them using properties of operations.
10	C	Number & Operations-Fractions	Understand a fraction $1/b$ as the quantity formed by 1 part when a whole is partitioned into b equal parts; understand a fraction a/b as the quantity formed by a parts of size $1/b$.
11	See Below	Number & Operations in Base Ten	Use place value understanding to round whole numbers to the nearest 10 or 100.
12	See Below	Operations/Algebraic Thinking	Use multiplication and division within 100 to solve word problems in situations involving equal groups, arrays, and measurement quantities.
13	See Below	Measurement & Data	Tell and write time to the nearest minute and measure time intervals in minutes. Solve word problems involving addition and subtraction of time intervals in minutes.
14	See Below	Number & Operations-Fractions	Recognize and generate simple equivalent fractions. Explain why the fractions are equivalent, e.g., by using a visual fraction model.
15	See Below	Measurement & Data	Solve real world and mathematical problems involving perimeters of polygons, including finding the perimeter given the side lengths, finding an unknown side length, and exhibiting rectangles with the same perimeter and different areas or with the same area and different perimeters.

Q11.
8,780 and 8,800

Explanation
The student should provide an explanation that refers to considering the number in the ones place when rounding to the nearest ten and considering the number in the tens place when rounding to the nearest hundred. The answer should include that the number is rounded down if the number is less than 5 and rounded up if the number is 5 or higher.

Scoring Information
Give a total score out of 4.
Give a score of 1 for each correct rounding.
Give a score out of 2 for the explanation.

Q12.
Answer
$6

Work
The work may show the division calculation $96 \div 16 = 6$. The work could use the missing factor equation $16 \times s = 96$.

Scoring Information
Give a total score out of 3.
Give a score of 1 for the correct answer.
Give a score out of 2 for the working.

Q13.
Answer
91 minutes

Work
The work may show calculating 25 minutes to 2 p.m., 60 minutes to 3 p.m., and 6 minutes to 3:06 p.m., and finding the sum of 25, 60, and 6. The work may show calculating 120 minutes from 1:35 to 3:35 and then subtracting (35 – 6) from 120. The work may show calculating 120 minutes from 3:06 to 1:06 and then subtracting (35 – 6) from 120. Other ways of calculating the elapsed time may also be accepted.

Scoring Information
Give a total score out of 3.
Give a score of 1 for the correct answer.
Give a score out of 2 for the working.

Q14.
Part A
The halves fraction bar should have 1 of the 2 segments shaded.
The quarters fraction bar should have 2 of the 4 segments shaded.

Part B
The eighths fraction bar should have 4 of the 8 segments shaded.

Answer
$\dfrac{4}{8}$

Scoring Information
Give a total score out of 4.
Give a score of 1 for each fraction bar correctly shaded.
Give a score of 1 for the correct answer in Part B.

Q15.
Part A
Answer
18 square units

Part B
The grid should have a 6 by 3 rectangle drawn on it.

Scoring Information
Give a total score out of 3.
Give a score of 1 for the correct answer in Part A.
Give a score of 2 for a 6 by 3 rectangle in Part B.
Give a score of 1 for a non-rectangular shape with an area of 18 square units.

PARCC Performance-Based Assessment, Practice Test 2, Session 2

Question	Answer	Topic	Common Core Skill
16	B	Measurement & Data	Draw a scaled picture graph to represent a data set with several categories.
17	D	Operations/Algebraic Thinking	Solve two-step word problems using the four operations.
18	$575	Number & Operations in Base Ten	Fluently add and subtract within 1000 using strategies and algorithms based on place value, properties of operations, and/or the relationship between addition and subtraction.
19	B	Operations/Algebraic Thinking	Fluently multiply and divide within 100. Know from memory all products of two one-digit numbers.
20	A	Measurement & Data	Solve real world and mathematical problems involving perimeters of polygons, including finding the perimeter given the side lengths.
21	See Below	Number & Operations in Base Ten	Use place value understanding to round whole numbers to the nearest 10 or 100.
22	See Below	Operations/Algebraic Thinking	Identify arithmetic patterns, and explain them using properties of operations.
23	See Below	Operations/Algebraic Thinking	Use multiplication and division within 100 to solve word problems in situations involving equal groups, arrays, and measurement quantities.
24	See Below	Measurement & Data	Recognize area as an attribute of plane figures and understand concepts of area measurement, including that a plane figure which can be covered without gaps or overlaps by n unit squares is said to have an area of n square units.
25	See Below	Number & Operations in Base Ten	Fluently add and subtract within 1000 using strategies and algorithms based on place value, properties of operations, and/or the relationship between addition and subtraction.
26	See Below	Measurement & Data	Draw a scaled bar graph to represent a data set with several categories. Solve one- and two-step "how many more" and "how many less" problems using information presented in scaled bar graphs.
27	See Below	Operations/Algebraic Thinking	Identify arithmetic patterns, and explain them using properties of operations.
28	See Below	Measurement & Data	Solve real world and mathematical problems involving perimeters of polygons, including finding the perimeter given the side lengths.
29	See Below	Number & Operations-Fractions	Recognize and generate simple equivalent fractions. Explain why the fractions are equivalent, e.g., by using a visual fraction model.
30	See Below	Number & Operations in Base Ten	Recognize that in a multi-digit whole number, a digit in one place represents ten times what it represents in the place to its right. Compare two multi-digit numbers based on meanings of the digits in each place.

Q21.
Part A
The number 48 should be plotted on the number line.

Part B
Answer
50

Explanation
The student should explain how you can tell that the number is closer to 50 than 40.

Scoring Information
Give a total score out of 3.
Give a score of 1 for the number correctly plotted in Part A.
Give a score of 1 for the correct answer in Part B.
Give a score out of 1 for the explanation.

Q22.
Answer
6 apple trees

Work
The work may show a division calculation such as 24 ÷ 4 or 30 ÷ 5. The work may also indicate that for every 1 more row added, there are another 6 apple trees.

Scoring Information
Give a total score out of 3.
Give a score of 1 for the correct answer.
Give a score out of 2 for the working.

Q23.
Answer
5 years

Work
The work should show the calculation of 60 ÷ 12 = 5 or 12 + 12 + 12 + 12 + 12 = 60.

Scoring Information
Give a total score out of 3.
Give a score of 1 for the correct answer.
Give a score out of 2 for the working.

Q24.
Answer
21 square centimeters

Work
The work should show that the student counted the number of squares. The work could show counting the number of whole squares and then the number of half squares. The work could involve dividing the shape into a rectangle and a triangle or a rectangle and two triangles. The work could also involve recognizing that the two triangles combine to form a 3 by 3 square.

Scoring Information
Give a total score out of 3.
Give a score of 1 for the correct answer.
Give a score out of 2 for the working.

Q25.
Answer
17

Work
The work should show the calculation of 45 − 28 = 17.

Scoring Information
Give a total score out of 3.
Give a score of 1 for the correct answer.
Give a score out of 2 for the working.

Q26.
Part A
The student should add a bar to 18 for Jan, a bar to 16 for Feb, and a bar to 14 for Mar.

Part B
Answer
$5

Work
The work could show the calculation of 19 − 14 = 5. or could use the graph to find the difference between the two bars.

Scoring Information
Give a total score out of 6.
Give a score of 1 for each bar correctly added in Part A.
Give a score of 1 for the correct answer in Part B.
Give a score out of 2 for the working in Part B.

Q27.
Answer
25

Explanation
The explanation should describe how each number in the pattern is 3 more than the number before it, and that the next number is found by adding 3 to 22.

Scoring Information
Give a total score out of 3.
Give a score of 1 for the correct answer.
Give a score out of 2 for the explanation.

Q28.
Answer
$532

Work
The work should show the calculation of the perimeter as 8 + 8 + 11 + 11 = 38 meters.
The work should show the calculation of the timber cost as 38 × 14 = 532.

Scoring Information
Give a total score out of 6.
Give a score of 1 for the correct perimeter found.
Give a score out of 2 for the working when finding the perimeter.
Give a score of 1 for the correct cost found.
Give a score out of 2 for the working when finding the cost.

Q29.
Part A
The model should have 3 parts of 18 shaded, or 1 part of 6 shaded, as shown below.

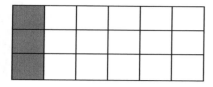 or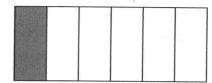

Part B
Answer
$\frac{1}{6}$

Work

The student may simplify $\frac{3}{18}$ to $\frac{1}{6}$. The student may also refer to using the model to determine the fraction, such as by explaining that 1 part of 6 total parts is shaded.

Scoring Information
Give a total score out of 4.
Give a score of 1 for the correct shading in Part A.
Give a score of 1 for the correct answer in Part B.
Give a score out of 2 for the working in Part B.

Q30.
Answer
146 and 164

Explanation
The explanation should refer to the place value of the numbers. It may describe how the number with the lowest value should be in the hundreds place.

Scoring Information
Give a total score out of 4.
Give a score of 1 for each correct number.
Give a score out of 2 for the explanation.

PARCC End-Of-Year Assessment, Practice Test 2, Session 1

Question	Answer	Topic	Common Core Skill
1	D	Number & Operations-Fractions	Understand a fraction 1/*b* as the quantity formed by 1 part when *a* whole is partitioned into *b* equal parts; understand a fraction *a*/*b* as the quantity formed by *a* parts of size 1/*b*.
2	Eva, Leah	Measurement & Data	Solve one- and two-step "how many more" and "how many less" problems using information presented in scaled bar graphs.
3	B	Operations/Algebraic Thinking	Solve two-step word problems using the four operations.
4	$27 \div 3 = 9$ $27 \div 9 = 3$	Operations/Algebraic Thinking	Interpret whole-number quotients of whole numbers, e.g., interpret $56 \div 8$ as the number of objects in each share when 56 objects are partitioned equally into 8 shares.
5	1st and 4th	Measurement & Data	Find areas of rectilinear figures by decomposing them into non-overlapping rectangles and adding the areas of the non-overlapping parts.
6	C	Operations/Algebraic Thinking	Solve two-step word problems using the four operations.
7	B	Operations/Algebraic Thinking	Identify arithmetic patterns, and explain them using properties of operations.
8	C	Operations/Algebraic Thinking	Assess the reasonableness of answers using mental computation and estimation strategies including rounding.
9	4 trees	Measurement & Data	Solve one- and two-step "how many more" and "how many less" problems using information presented in scaled bar graphs.
10	B	Operations/Algebraic Thinking	Solve two-step word problems using the four operations.
11	$6 + 5 + 6 + 5$ $= 22$ $2(6 + 5) = 22$	Measurement & Data	Solve real world and mathematical problems involving perimeters of polygons, including finding the perimeter given the side lengths.
12	D	Geometry	Partition shapes into parts with equal areas. Express the area of each part as a unit fraction of the whole.
13	C	Operations/Algebraic Thinking	Fluently multiply and divide within 100. Know from memory all products of two one-digit numbers.
14	20, 30, 40	Number & Operations in Base Ten	Use place value understanding to round whole numbers to the nearest 10 or 100.
15	$\frac{2}{8} = \frac{1}{4}$	Number & Operations-Fractions	Recognize and generate simple equivalent fractions. Explain why the fractions are equivalent, e.g., by using a visual fraction model.
16	A	Number & Operations-Fractions	Understand a fraction as a number on the number line; represent fractions on a number line diagram.
17	B	Operations/Algebraic Thinking	Interpret products of whole numbers, e.g., interpret 5×7 as the total number of objects in 5 groups of 7 objects each.
18	8 pizzas	Operations/Algebraic Thinking	Use multiplication and division within 100 to solve word problems in situations involving equal groups, arrays, and measurement quantities.

19	40 ÷ 8 = 5 or 40 ÷ 5 = 8	Operations/Algebraic Thinking	Fluently multiply and divide within 100, using strategies such as the relationship between multiplication and division or properties of operations.
20	C	Measurement & Data	Measure and estimate masses of objects.
21	D	Measurement & Data	Solve real world and mathematical problems involving perimeters of polygons, including finding the perimeter given the side lengths.
22	36	Operations/Algebraic Thinking	Identify arithmetic patterns, and explain them using properties of operations.
23	C	Geometry	Recognize rhombuses, rectangles, and squares as examples of quadrilaterals.
24	C	Operations/Algebraic Thinking	Identify arithmetic patterns, and explain them using properties of operations.
25	A	Operations/Algebraic Thinking	Apply properties of operations as strategies to multiply and divide, including the distributive property.

PARCC End-Of-Year Assessment, Practice Test 2, Session 2

Question	Answer	Topic	Common Core Skill
26	2nd and 4th	Operations/Algebraic Thinking	Use multiplication and division within 100 to solve word problems in situations involving equal groups, arrays, and measurement quantities.
27	8 emails	Measurement & Data	Draw a scaled picture graph to represent a data set with several categories.
28	B	Measurement & Data	Tell and write time to the nearest minute and measure time intervals in minutes.
29	D	Measurement & Data	Multiply side lengths to find areas of rectangles with whole-number side lengths in the context of solving real world and mathematical problems.
30	A	Measurement & Data	Draw a scaled picture graph to represent a data set with several categories.
31	C	Measurement & Data	Add, subtract, multiply, or divide to solve one-step word problems involving masses or volumes that are given in the same units.
32	Any 2 of the 8 squares shaded	Number & Operations-Fractions	Recognize and generate simple equivalent fractions. Explain why the fractions are equivalent, e.g., by using a visual fraction model.
33	336 students	Operations/Algebraic Thinking	Fluently multiply and divide within 100, using strategies such as the relationship between multiplication and division or properties of operations.
34	B	Measurement & Data	Generate measurement data by measuring lengths using rulers marked with halves and fourths of an inch.
35	C	Operations/Algebraic Thinking	Understand division as an unknown-factor problem.
36	B	Measurement & Data	Tell and write time to the nearest minute and measure time intervals in minutes.
37	A	Number & Operations-Fractions	Record the results of comparisons with the symbols >, =, or <, and justify the conclusions, e.g., by using a visual fraction model.
38	C	Operations/Algebraic Thinking	Interpret products of whole numbers, e.g., interpret 5×7 as the total number of objects in 5 groups of 7 objects each.
39	10, 14, 28	Operations/Algebraic Thinking	Use multiplication and division within 100 to solve word problems in situations involving equal groups, arrays, and measurement quantities.
40	20, 32, 44	Operations/Algebraic Thinking	Interpret products of whole numbers, e.g., interpret 5×7 as the total number of objects in 5 groups of 7 objects each.
41	B	Operations/Algebraic Thinking	Solve two-step word problems using the four operations.
42	2, 3, 1, 4	Number & Operations-Fractions	Compare two fractions with the same numerator or the same denominator by reasoning about their size.
43	A	Operations/Algebraic Thinking	Use multiplication and division within 100 to solve word problems in situations involving equal groups, arrays, and measurement quantities.
44	C	Operations/Algebraic Thinking	Solve two-step word problems using the four operations.
45	$\frac{4}{2}, \frac{8}{4}$	Number & Operations-Fractions	Express whole numbers as fractions, and recognize fractions that are equivalent to whole numbers.

46	D	Measurement & Data	Draw a scaled picture graph to represent a data set with several categories.
47	$\frac{3}{6}$ and $\frac{6}{12}$	Number & Operations-Fractions	Recognize and generate simple equivalent fractions.
48	Dean: kite Selma: triangle	Geometry	Understand that shapes in different categories (e.g., rhombuses, rectangles, and others) may share attributes (e.g., having four sides), and that the shared attributes can define a larger category (e.g., quadrilaterals).
49	B	Measurement & Data	Solve real world and mathematical problems involving perimeters of polygons, including finding the perimeter given the side lengths.
50	C	Measurement & Data	Measure and estimate masses of objects.

Made in the USA
Middletown, DE
15 March 2016